SIRSHREE

THE MIRACLE OF GRATITUDE

Whispers of Thanks
Echoes of Wonder

The Miracle of Gratitude
Whispers of Thanks, Echoes of Wonder

By **Sirshree** Tejparkhi

Copyright © Tejgyan Global Foundation
All Rights Reserved 2025

Tejgyan Global Foundation is a charitable organization
with its headquarters in Pune, India.

ISBN : 978-93-90132-77-5

Published by WOW Publishings Pvt. Ltd., India

First edition published in March 2025

Printed and bound by Trinity Academy For Corporate Training Ltd, Pune

This book is based on the Hindi book titled,
The Miracle of Gratitude by Sirshree Tejparkhi

Copyright and publishing rights are vested exclusively with WOW Publishings Pvt. Ltd. This book is sold subject to the condition that it shall not by way of trade or otherwise, be lent, resold, hired out, or otherwise circulated without the publisher's prior written consent in any form of binding or cover other than that in which it is published and without a similar condition including this condition being imposed on the subsequent purchaser and without limiting the rights under copyright reserved above, no part of this publication may be reproduced, stored in or introduced into a retrieval system, or transmitted, in any form, or by any means, electronic, mechanical, photocopying, recording or otherwise, without the prior written permission of both the copyright owner and the above-mentioned publisher of this book. Any person who does any unauthorized act in relation to this publication may be liable to criminal prosecution and civil claims for damages.

Although the author and publisher have made every effort to ensure accuracy of content in this book, they hereby disclaim any liability to any party for any loss, damage, or disruption caused by errors or omissions, resulting from negligence, accident, or any other cause. Readers are advised to take full responsibility to exercise discretion in understanding and applying the content of this book.

Heartfelt gratitude…

To all the sanitation workers of the world,
whose tireless efforts preserve the beauty and cleanliness of the Earth,
contributing immensely to the physical and mental well-being of all.

To all those whom you are grateful for

(write down their names.)

Gratitude! Gratitude! Gratitude!

Content

Preface - The Secret of Nature's Generosity	7
Introduction - Feel Thankful	9
PART 1 - Gratitude The First Necessity of Life	**13**
1. Thank You – a Spiritual Experience	15
2. The Realization of Gratitude	19
3. Gratitude – the Foundation of Life	23
4. Gratitude – a Powerful Vibration	28
5. Associate Feeling with Gratitude	31
6. Freedom From a Life of Complaints	36
7. Wearing the Cloak of Gratitude	41
8. Perceiving Virtues with Gratitude	46
PART 2 - The Glory of Gratitude and its Practice	**51**
9. The Science of Gratitude	53
10. The Importance of Gratitude in Action	59
11. Thanking The Three Aspects of God	64
12. Embrace the Abundance of Nature	69
13. The Invisible Law Within Gratitude	74
14. The Importance of Purity in Gratitude	80
15. The Role of Faith in Gratitude	84
PART 3 - When and Whom to Thank	**87**
16. Be Grateful for Your Body	89
17. Gratitude Meditation for the Body	93
18. Gratitude for the Tools That Serve Us	99
19. Gratitude for Those Who Teach Us How to Live	106

20. Instilling Gratitude in Children	112
21. Being Grateful for Undesirable Events	118
22. Gratitude for Prosperity	125
23. Attracting Qualities Through Gratitude	132

PART 4 - From Gratitude Toward Supreme Gratitude — 137

24. Let Gratitude Become a Way of Life	139
25. Celebrate Thanksgiving Every Day	144
26. Moving toward Supreme Gratitude	146
27. Surrender, Fulfillment, and Gratitude	149
28. Meditation on Reasons for Gratitude	153
29. The Gratitude Mantra, Bank, and Journal	159
30. A Gratitude Letter from the Future You	161
Appendix	167

Preface

The Secret of Nature's Generosity

How often have you expressed heartfelt gratitude in your life? Have you reflected on the profound impact that gratitude can have? Have you experienced how expressing gratitude sweetens your relationships? Do you believe that daily gratitude can augment your happiness and satisfaction? Have you felt peace by expressing gratitude even for the most trivial things?

Yes! We all have experienced the superficial benefits of gratitude but its impact is far more profound. When we say, "Thank you," we not only acknowledge someone's help but also send a powerful vibration of gratitude into the Universe, positively affecting ourselves and those around us. It is no wonder that all the great scriptures, sages, and saints across religions have glorified the greatness of gratitude.

Yet, some might wonder, "What's so special about expressing gratitude all the time? Isn't saying 'Thank you' just a formality?" The following story illustrates this.

> An old farmer would look at the produce of his field every day and thank it. One day, his neighbor curiously inquired, "Why do you do this, especially when bad weather could ruin your crops completely?" The farmer smiled, "I'm grateful for whatever I receive, whether less

or more. Gratitude fortifies my soul and inspires me to persevere patiently, even in adversity." Because of this mindset, the farmer never felt any lack in his life.

This short story illustrates the simple yet profound impact of gratitude, which inspires us to remain balanced and positive in every situation. When we express gratitude for even the most trivial incidents in life, no matter how ordinary they may seem, we experience incredible joy.

You might wonder whether gratitude has its own language. There are countless languages and dialects spoken across the world in which people offer their prayers. Yet, they are all answered. How does it happen? Does Nature understand all these languages and maintain an account of everyone? Not really! It is not language that matters for Nature but the vibrations of heartfelt feelings.

It is not what you say but what you feel that makes things happen. For example, when you receive something you desire, you say "Thank you," which means you are in the "Yes, I have" feeling. Similarly, when you desire something you do not have and still express gratitude for it, the Universe does not respond to your words but to your feeling of "Yes, I have it." This is the secret of Nature's generosity.

Imagine a child insisting on a toy before going to bed. The father assures the child, "I will bring you the toy tomorrow." Hearing this, the child happily falls asleep, feeling assured they already have it. Seeing the child's happiness, the father indeed fulfills the promise and brings the toy the next day.

The point is that everything, whether a toy or divine grace, is waiting to come into our lives. We need to start living in the feeling of "Yes, I have," with joy and gratitude. Begin reading this book with that feeling.

When we understand the merit of gratitude and harmonize with Nature by being thankful, the flow of life leads us toward success, happiness, devotion, and contentment.

Introduction

Feel Thankful

Once upon a time, a deer in a jungle unknowingly consumed something poisonous which spread throughout her body. Her once vibrant form became frail. She struggled to move around and find food for her fawns. The ill effect of the poison made her stumble and fall, making it even harder to care for her young ones. She was worried about how she would care for herself and her fawns.

One day, an elephant passed by while she was lost in sorrow and distress. He noticed that the usually cheerful deer, known for her playful leaps, seemed shattered. The elephant curiously approached her and inquired, "What has happened to you?"

The deer, with a heavy heart, replied, "I have accidentally consumed something poisonous. It is causing me immense pain and suffering."

After listening to her story, the elephant consoled her, "Just follow what I tell you. My master taught me certain principles that I adhere to strictly, and you should too."

The deer felt relieved to receive sympathy and asked, "What did your master teach you?"

The elephant shared his story: "A mahout raised me from an early age. He inscribed something on my body in a human language, which I couldn't read, but he would sing it to me as a lullaby: '**Feel Thankful. Be grateful.**'

"He taught me from the beginning to always thank God. He was always cheerful and joyful. Even when something bad happened, the brightness on his face and his happiness never dimmed. He would always say, '**Be thankful for everything—for what you have and what you don't.** Someone is watching over us, giving us what we need. Accept it and be thankful.' He always thanked God for making him human and taught me, even as an animal, to do the same.

"As he grew old, I grew up. His body remained small, but mine grew enormous. He continued to teach me: '**Your body is big, and mine is small.** Thanks for that. There are things you can do that I cannot. Thanks for that, too. There are things I can do that you cannot. Thanks for that. Thank you… Thank you… Thank you…'

"My master raised me with these teachings. When it was time for him to leave this world, he told me, 'Now, you must go into the jungle and live a free and joyful life.' Following his last wish, I live happily in the jungle and still follow his teachings. Every day, I roam joyfully.

"Now, like me, you should start thanking for what you have. Be thankful for your fawns. Be thankful that you can still stand and walk. Even when you stumble, be thankful for the ability to get up and walk again. Thank your legs. Start practicing this consistently. I must go now, but will check on you upon my return." Saying this, the elephant moved on.

A few days later, when the elephant returned, he saw that the entire atmosphere had changed. The deer was happily living with her fawns, and many more deer had joined them, forming a large herd. They were joyfully leaping and playing. The once-ill deer was now full of energy and courage. Surprised, the elephant asked, "Wow! You look so happy. How did this miracle happen?"

The deer excitedly narrated, "The day you taught me about gratitude, something stirred within me. From that moment until night, I repeated, 'Thank you... thank you...' and fell asleep with the same feeling. I woke up feeling a positive transformation within me. I realized that giving thanks had spread a vibration of happiness throughout my body, healing something within me. This strengthened my faith in gratitude, and I continued the practice.

"The next day, I fell while gathering food. At that moment, a new thought arose, 'Thank you for making me fall.' Immediately, I felt a surge of awareness. I got up and brought food for my fawns. I felt as if I had discovered a magic wand in the form of gratitude. I decided to thank for everything, as if waving this magic wand.

"This practice continued. As I whispered thanks, Nature echoed its wonders. More deer joined and helped me. Gradually, the joy and gratitude healed my body, and our herd also grew. Today, I am completely healthy, happily waving the magic wand of gratitude. I am deeply grateful to you for giving me this magic wand!"

This story explains the power of gratitude. We should also fill our minds with gratitude. When our minds are filled with negativity, it affects our bodies with illness, fatigue, and burdens. Gratitude is the key! It brings joy, which heals negative thoughts and emotions. When we feel gratitude, we naturally feel joyful, and our pain begins to heal. If we fall asleep every night feeling grateful, we wake up feeling healed and well.

At first, you might feel mechanical when expressing thanks. You might wonder, "What's the need to say thank you repeatedly?" But persistence is the key. Only through constant practice will the genuine feeling of gratitude awaken within you. To move forward from where you are today and raise your level of consciousness, the simplest yet most powerful way is to keep giving thanks.

Give thanks for everything that happens according to your wishes. Even when things don't go your way, thank God, for whatever happened was according to the divine will, and the reason behind it is yet to be revealed.

There are two types of people in this world: those who live with gratitude and those who live with a sense of lack. Grateful people find reasons to be thankful, regardless of circumstances. On the other hand, those who live in lack, even when good things happen, keep wondering, "Will things continue to go well?" And when bad things happen, it reinforces their negative beliefs.

Reflect on how you want your life to be—a blessing or a curse, grateful or ungrateful, complaining or counting blessings.

When genuine gratitude awakens, you feel assured that whatever you need will manifest effortlessly and naturally. Therefore, learn to give thanks despite challenges, worries, and illnesses so your level of consciousness rises, and you reach the heights of joy.

PART 1

Gratitude
The First Necessity of Life

After each part, there is an illustration, silent yet powerful, awaiting your words of gratitude. It is a canvas you can fill with the expressions of your heart and decorate with the colors that speak to you most. These illustrations represent the language of the right brain—a creative, intuitive way of offering prayers to Nature. By embracing this practice, you will fill your life with gratitude and boundless joy.

1

Thank You – a Spiritual Experience

*"Feeling gratitude and not expressing it
is like wrapping a gift and not giving it."*
- William Arthur Ward

Once, a farmer was sitting alone by a riverside in a very miserable state. Just then, a saint happened to pass by. Sensing the farmer's distress, he compassionately inquired, "My child, what troubles you? Why do you sit here in such despair?"

Tears rolled down his cheeks as the farmer recounted his misfortunes. "My life is shattered. My home and land are mortgaged. I have no money to feed my family, no work to earn a living, and no way to relieve my suffering. I am tired of fighting the relentless challenges of life. I can't bear this suffering anymore. I see no other way but to end my life."

The saint intently listened to him and calmly replied, "If you have determined to end your life, do it tomorrow. But give me your time today. Come with me."

The saint took the farmer to a wealthy merchant. He first spoke to the merchant in private and then turning to the farmer, he said, "This wealthy merchant says that since you have resolved to end your life tomorrow, you might as well give him one of your eyes. He lost his own and will pay you a fair price."

Startled, the farmer immediately recoiled, "No! I can't give up my eye."

"No problem!" the saint continued. "If you can't give your eye, perhaps you can consider giving one of your kidneys. The merchant's father is gravely ill and in desperate need of one. You will be well compensated."

The farmer, disapprovingly, protested, "I have two children. Who will look after them? I can't give up my kidney!"

"But you are planning to end your life tomorrow anyway," the saint gently reminded him. "Then why are you worrying about your eye and kidney?"

The conversation continued for some time, but the farmer refused to part with any of his body parts despite the generous offers. Gradually, he began to realize the value of his body.

The merchant then revealed the secret. "Many years ago, my situation was like yours," he confessed. "Overwhelmed by insurmountable problems, I was about to end my life. But this very saint guided me and saved my life. I now live a happy and prosperous life."

The farmer was stunned. He thought, "I believed I was the only one undergoing such suffering. However, thousands like me have been through this path of despair, only to emerge into a life of abundance through guidance."

He realized that instead of contemplating suicide, he should be working hard, and, above all, be grateful to God for giving him the precious gift of life.

"Thank you, God, for everything I have today," he whispered. "Thank You… Thank You… Thank You…" He felt the grace of God bestowed upon him. His heart overflowed with gratitude. He fell at the feet of the saint. "Revered saint, you have opened my eyes to the true value of life. Blinded by my suffering, I was about to make a terrible mistake. You saved me."

The saint made the farmer realize that his life, with all its challenges, was far more precious than he had ever imagined. This profound understanding gave birth to gratitude.

Like the farmer, we often yearn for what we lack and fail to appreciate the countless treasures we already possess. This is the root cause of our distress. We have eyes to see, a nose to smell, a tongue to taste and speak. However, if we lack a house, we obsess over it. If we have a home, we crave a better job. If we have a job, we want a good car, and so on.

This scarcity mindset causes life's blessings to slip through our fingers and drift away. But when we embrace the feeling of "Yes, I have" for what we have, we experience abundance, and the best things of the universe come into our lives.

Therefore, we should change our perspective: "Even though my house is small, I have a roof over my head. Even though I cannot afford to dine in expensive restaurants, I have two meals daily. I have clothes to wear. I have received a good education. God has given me two hands, legs, and eyes to experience the world. I am blessed."

The "Yes, I have" feeling is in essence the feeling of gratitude. When we embrace this feeling, life starts to flow harmoniously. Things start coming into our lives easily and our problems begin to get solved. Otherwise, the habit of living in a state of lack keeps us away from everyday happiness. However, this mindset can be changed when we learn to be grateful for what we have received.

The Miracle of Gratitude - 17

Today, many people have realized the importance of focusing on "What they want," but the feeling of gratitude transcends the realm of material gain and loss. It trains our subconscious mind, anchoring us in the feeling of "Yes, I have," welcoming abundance with open arms.

Gratitude is a magnetic feeling that makes us receptive to all the positive things in the universe. It brings a smile to our faces. It is faith in action. It is like planting a seed for the future, knowing it will surely grow. We are confident that it is bound to happen; it has already happened. This innate sense of gratitude has been within us since childhood, but over time, it got obscured by the dark clouds of adverse experiences. Some doubts and disappointments have gathered dust on it. But now, the time has come to rediscover it by clearing away this dust with understanding, contemplation, and purposeful action.

Gratitude is also about knowing that the world is replete with many beautiful and good things. It is the feeling that Nature has generously bestowed upon us countless gifts, often without our asking, that have seamlessly become a part of our lives. It is about acknowledging that something around us is making our lives richer, easier, and more delightful. With this recognition, we feel grateful and embrace grace.

The word "Gratitude" finds its roots in the Latin term "*gratus*," which means to be thankful for the people and things that have enriched our lives and made it beautiful. At its core, gratitude is recognizing the value of life's blessings.

Every language has its own way of expressing this profound feeling: *Meherbani, Shukraan, Dhanyawad, Kritagyata, Shukriya, Aabhar,* Thanks, Gratitude, Gracias, Gratefulness, Danke, Dankie, Merci, Grazie, Obrigado.

When we say "Thank you" to someone, we acknowledge them, express gratitude for their actions, and feel a sense of indebtedness. We use these words to convey their importance in our lives, making them happy and inspiring to continue their good work.

Points for Contemplation:

- Contemplate how the farmer's realization applies to your life.
- What exactly does it mean to be in the "Yes, I have" feeling?

2

The Realization of Gratitude

*"The worship most acceptable to God comes
from a thankful and cheerful heart."*
- Plutarch

A guru and his disciple would travel from village to village, preaching spiritual wisdom. They would journey for eight months of the year and return to their hermitage during the four-month monsoon season when all the roads would be blocked due to flooded rivers and streams, making travel difficult. Many sages and saints still follow this tradition, known as *Chaturmas* when they confine themselves to one place for the monsoon season.

As one summer drew to a close, they began their journey back to their hermitage. After walking some distance, they were caught in a fierce storm. The torrential rain drenched them completely, forcing them to seek shelter under a tree. With its howling winds and relentless rain, the violent storm threatened to destroy everything in its path.

When the storm finally subsided, they continued to their lakeside hermitage. As they approached, they discovered the storm had torn off half of the roof and uprooted several trees. Their already small hermitage had become even smaller. The distant thunder warned of impending rain. The night was closing in, and with the storm still threatening, they could neither repair the roof nor find shelter

elsewhere. They were left to spend the night in their damaged dwelling.

Exhausted from their journey and having not eaten since morning, the disciple was bewildered by the scenario. Frustrated, he grumbled, "Look at this, the very God we venerate day and night subjects us to such trials. We live virtuous lives, yet we don't even have a peaceful place to sleep."

The guru silently ignored the disciple and began cleaning the hermitage. Meanwhile, the disciple stood outside, seething with resentment. He thought, "What's the point of prayer and meditation if this is our fate? The rich, greedy, and even sinful sleep peacefully in their homes, while we renunciates don't even have a roof to protect us. What kind of justice is this?"

Eventually, the disciple calmed down and entered the hermitage. To his surprise, he saw his guru standing with folded hands immersed in silent reverence. His face was radiant with joy and tears streamed down his cheeks. He gazed up at the sky and spoke with a heart overflowing with gratitude, "O God, Your mercy knows no bounds. You spared half of our shelter from the wrath of the storm. You are so kind and caring for all."

The guru and disciple confronted the same adversity, yet their responses were worlds apart. While the guru exuded joy and gratitude, the disciple was consumed with complaints and discontent.

Exhausted from their arduous journey, both lay down to rest. The guru immediately drifted off to sleep, but the disciple tossed and turned throughout the night, plagued by anxiety. He feared, "What if the rest of the roof collapses? What if it rains again? What if the storm returns?"

When he finally dozed off for a while, his mind was still filled with anguish and complaints, even in his dreams. On the other hand, the guru slept peacefully, untroubled by the chaos around him.

At dawn, the guru awoke and saw the moon shining brightly in the sky through the ruptured roof. He marveled at the celestial spectacle, praising God for the experience. "O God," he exclaimed.

"Had I known that sleeping under a broken roof was so exhilarating, I would have dismantled it myself! I wouldn't have troubled You for a storm. Now I see the breathtaking beauty of the sky and the moon, that was hidden from me by my sturdy roof."

One who remains steadfast in the face of adversity, neither fearing nor complaining, never thinks, "Something bad has happened or will happen." Instead, a wellspring of gratitude and prayer arises within them. This clearly demonstrates that the guru had attained something that allowed him to remain perpetually joyful, regardless of external circumstances.

Whatever seeds of emotion we sow today will inevitably bear fruit in the coming days. Do you aspire to be like the guru, balanced and joyful in all circumstances? If so, embrace this opportunity and cultivate gratitude in your life.

Just as wild shrubs and grasses grow in an untended forest, so does our mind. Without conscious effort, our mind tends to gravitate toward negative thoughts and patterns. However, if we consciously cultivate positive thoughts, we can transform our mental landscape into a vibrant and flourishing garden that can spread the fragrance of love and joy to everyone around us.

Now, reflect on how the guru could maintain a state of joy and gratitude, even amid adversity. What insights enabled him to attain such a state of grace? What had he achieved that his disciple still lacked?

The Miracle of Gratitude

The guru had attained an elevated state of consciousness. He had realized the immense power of gratitude and was immersed in its bliss. He had truly understood and integrated gratitude into his being.

Gratitude is about awakening love for God, the supreme consciousness, and being grateful for whatever is happening in the present moment. This profound sense of love fosters faith. When gratitude arises out of love and faith, it has the power to transform one's entire being. It purifies the mind, dissolves the ego, transcending the limited individual being.

It is easy to say "Thank you" when things happen according to our wishes. But true gratitude arises when we appreciate life's blessings even during challenging times. It is far more than just casually saying "Thank you." It is a profound, heartfelt emotion that naturally emerges when we deeply contemplate the blessings bestowed upon us, connecting us to divine consciousness.

We are a minuscule part of this vast universe, yet an unseen force is watching over us, caring for us every moment. We have done nothing for this beautiful nature, yet everything manifests on its own. Nature is brimming with love and joy, abundantly providing for us endlessly. This realization cultivates a profound sense of gratitude within us.

In the following chapters, we will delve deeper into the significance of gratitude and how to integrate it into our daily lives. Drawing inspiration from the story of the guru and his disciple, we will also learn to cultivate a habit of gratitude and witness its profound impact on our lives.

Points for Contemplation:

- When faced with the same challenges, what differentiated the guru's response from that of the disciple?
- How could the guru maintain a state of joy and gratitude, even amid adversity?
- What insights can you draw from the guru's state of grace? How can you integrate that perspective in your life?

3

Gratitude – the Foundation of Life

"Gratitude unlocks the fullness of life. It turns what we have into enough and more. It turns denial into acceptance, chaos to order, confusion to clarity. Gratitude makes sense of our past, brings peace for today, and creates a vision for tomorrow."
- Melody Beattie

Once, there was a hunter. He was so skilled in archery that it seemed as if the very art of archery, passed down to him as a legacy, was fascinated by him. His unparalleled skill provided sustenance for his family, for which he was eternally grateful.

One day, when he heard about a government ban on hunting, he was shaken. The thought of his family's survival filled him with dread. But as soon as his gaze fell upon the bow slung across his shoulder, a spark of hope ignited within him, and a gentle smile emerged. He felt grateful for his archery skills and the legacy of his ancestors. As he had good knowledge about the forest, he harnessed his archery skills to gather wild vegetables, fruits, and roots to sustain his family. Despite the adversity, the hunter and his family remained thankful for what they had.

One day, while fetching water from a lake, the hunter chanced upon a family from the city enjoying a leisurely picnic. Suddenly, a ferocious wild animal pounced on their small puppy. With lightning speed and precision, the hunter shot an arrow, compelling the beast to flee and miraculously saving the puppy unharmed.

The head of the family was utterly astonished by the hunter's incredible skill. He profusely thanked the hunter and invited him to participate in an upcoming archery competition in the city. Without a moment's hesitation, the hunter accepted the challenge and entered the contest. To the astonishment of all, he emerged victorious, claiming the gold medal. His exceptional performance left the spectators awestruck.

Shortly thereafter, a renowned sports club in the city, recognizing his exceptional talent, appointed him to teach archery to their students. He dedicated the rest of his life to sharing his archery skills and imparting the profound wisdom of gratitude.

The essence of the story underscores a powerful truth: Even in the face of seemingly insurmountable challenges, by remaining grateful for what we have, we can easily unveil hidden gifts within the garb of the adversity, transforming challenges into opportunities.

When we express gratitude for something, our focus naturally shifts toward it. The law of focus states that **what we focus on grows.** However, a deeper truth lies beneath this: Things do not grow simply because we focus on them. Our attention is a spark emanating from our consciousness—the awareness within each of us. This awareness is the real creator, the force behind all manifestation. The power of gratitude ignites this spark, awakening the creative power within us.

From a scientific perspective, expressing gratitude brings about positive changes in the brain. It stimulates the secretion of feel-good neurotransmitters like dopamine and serotonin, instantly uplifting our mood and enhancing our overall well-being. This harmonious interplay of happiness and the profound sense of abundance arising from the feeling of "Yes, I have" fuels the creative process. Gratitude is the foundation of all creation.

The hunter and his family exemplify the true essence of gratitude. In this state, by expressing gratitude for all they had, their life was perpetually filled with joy, peace, and contentment. Thus, one can experience lasting happiness by fostering a heartfelt sense of thankfulness.

Our ancestors revered the glory of gratitude as depicted in the ancient scriptures. In the Indian epic Mahabharata, when Lord Krishna slew Shishupala with his Sudarshan Chakra, his finger was injured and began to bleed. In a moment of pure love and devotion, Draupadi tore a piece from her saree and gently wrapped it around Lord Krishna's wound, grateful for the chance to serve him. Deeply touched by this selfless act, Lord Krishna blessed her with the promise, "I will always be with you." True to his word, Lord Krishna stood by Draupadi in every crisis, protecting her at every turn. That single act of gratitude became a wellspring of eternal protection and love, a divine blessing for her entire life.

In Indian culture, the sacred practice of rituals and prayers is used to thank God and nature. While gratitude does not require a set time, certain times of the day are emphasized for reflection and thanksgiving. For instance, one should offer gratitude to Nature upon waking up and thank God for everything received and not received* during the day before going to bed at night. In some countries, Thanksgiving is celebrated with family and friends, involving feasts and sharing gratitude for the blessings in life.

When we immerse ourselves in nature's embrace, surrounded by majestic mountains, flowing rivers, boundless oceans, or beneath the vast expanse of the sky, our hearts overflow with joy and a profound sense of appreciation. We experience deep love and an unparalleled inner peace. These feelings naturally blossom into an expression of gratitude.

The power of gratitude is boundless. It brings profound transformation and fulfillment into our lives. Just as breath sustains our physical body, gratitude nourishes our inner being, welcoming grace and blessings.

---

*Why should we be grateful even for what we have not received? Explore this in Chapter 21, Page 118

A Testimonial of Gratitude

2019 was the most challenging year of my life. All the deep-seated emotions buried in my subconscious since childhood erupted like a volcano. The lava that spewed out engulfed my entire being. My physical health deteriorated. What began as a bout of white jaundice transformed into the more serious condition of Hepatitis B. The looming fear of losing my job due to my illness compounded my distress. My body's weakness and my mind's helplessness pushed me to the edge of despair. I even started to contemplate suicide.

I had received teachings from my guru about "Gratitude, Acceptance, and Letting Go," but had not truly understood and imbibed them. One fateful day, I reached an unbearable low and thought, "I cannot endure this any longer. I must do something today to commit suicide!"

Then, I came across my guru's powerful message about the transformative power of gratitude. He said, "All prayers are answered; simply express gratitude in every situation. Whatever event or illness you are experiencing has come only to leave."

This revelation struck me like a divine spark. I suddenly understood that my prayers for good health had been heard. The illnesses that plagued me were not a curse but a catalyst for my ultimate healing. They had arisen solely to exit my body, clearing the path for my well-being.

With this newfound clarity, my mind overflowed with gratitude. Tears of devotion streaming down my face washed away all the negative thoughts in my mind. Day and night, I prayed fervently and thanked God. "My body is now fully healthy, vibrant, and strong. Thank you, God, for this healing!" I visualized my body, renewed and revitalized. Soon, it became a reality.

The journey from suicide to self-liberation became possible only through the power of gratitude. Today, besides physical and mental health, I have attained wellness in all aspects of my life. My existence that once felt trapped in inner turmoil, conflict, and emotional strife has blossomed into a harmonious inner dialog, all thanks to the grace of gratitude.

- A seeker of Truth

Points for Contemplation:

- What are the skills you have inherited from your ancestors, your family? Be grateful for them.
- Where do you generally focus on—the lack of things or abundance?
- Look around you and notice the blessings bestowed by Nature right now.

4

Gratitude – a Powerful Vibration

"I would maintain that thanks are the highest form of thought and that gratitude is happiness doubled by wonder."
- G.K. Chesterton

When we silently thank someone, we feel heartfelt gratitude for their cooperation. Even without expressing thanks verbally, the positive vibration of our gratitude reaches their subconscious mind. The next time we encounter them, they feel good in our presence. In other words, the feeling of gratitude is such an elevated vibration that holds the power to transform the entire world positively.

Regardless of who we are, where we are, and our current circumstances, living with gratitude, we can change our circumstances and society.

When one returns home stressed after a long day, one's irritable behavior can disturb the entire family. Just as stress creates even more stress, and happiness spreads more of itself, so does the feeling of gratitude. The habit of being thankful inspires many others. In a particular tradition, when someone says thanks for receiving help, they are told, "Don't say thank you. Help three more people." Soon, this chain of gratitude and goodwill spreads throughout society.

If we nurture the habit of being thankful, this habit creates a ripple effect, spreading positivity and bringing about a transformative change across society and the world, benefitting everyone.

A Testimonial of Gratitude

Since childhood, I have been saying "Thank you." But I believed I should use these words only when someone helps me. However, when I gained an understanding of the truth of life, I began to unravel the essence of gratitude in depth.

Initially, I had to put in conscious effort to practice gratitude. I began to notice details of my surroundings which I had previously overlooked. I used to walk past the sanitation worker cleaning my society's path daily without noticing her. During this newfound practice of gratitude, awareness awakened within me, and one morning, I saw the sanitation worker sweeping diligently without a mask, struggling with the dust. I asked, "Why don't you wear a mask? This could make you ill!"

She explained that she could not afford to buy one. Without a second thought, I took out a new mask from my bag and gave it to her. Her face immediately lit up with joy that touched my heart. Folding her hands in gratitude, she said, "So many people have passed by here since morning, but no one paid attention. You noticed me and cared for my well-being. If only everyone showed a little more compassion."

Without hesitation, I replied, "Thank you for working so hard and keeping our society clean. It's our responsibility to take care of your health and well-being." That day, I felt the power of gratitude. As she put on the mask, there was a noticeable change in her work. Words cannot describe the energy and joy she exuded as she worked. Now, she was brimming with enthusiasm in her work. Alongside her renewed sense of purpose, I felt an unspoken bond grew between us.

A few days later, when I went to the market, the same woman was calling out to me from the other side of the road, saying a warm "Hello." Her voice caught my attention. When I turned to see her, she waved her hand with a smile that radiated happiness. Now, wherever we meet, we greet each other with a smile. A simple "Thank you" had brought us unexpected joy. Along with gratitude, I learned the profound value of appreciation. The vibration of my appreciation touched her, making her enthusiastic and energetic toward her work.

- A seeker of Truth

This is not about giving a mask but demonstrating the remarkable power of gratitude in action. When we express gratitude, the flow of energy becomes positive. When we say "Thank you" not as a mere formality but to sincerely express heartfelt gratitude, its positive vibrations uplift others. When we thank someone with love, their quality of work improves. Any work done with joy naturally reaches a higher standard. Expressing gratitude to anyone working in our vicinity creates a wellspring of inspiration for them.

Imagine a homemaker who serves her family selflessly every day. She tirelessly cooks meals for her family, prepares her children for school, and manages the household. Yet, if her family overlooks her efforts or takes it for granted, she may feel discouraged. Tasks performed in such a discouraged state do not yield good results. However, if she receives a little appreciation for all she does, perhaps a few words of thanks, a compliment for a dish she cooked, or a helping hand, she will feel happy and motivated to perform her tasks with a renewed positive energy. This will create a warm and harmonious atmosphere at home.

Similarly, we should thank our colleagues in the workplace. Their support and collaboration enable us to accomplish our work. For those who do not cooperate, we should silently thank them, thinking, "They are making me independent and patient." Moreover, we should pat ourselves on the back, thinking, "The feeling of gratitude is awakening within me. I can even thank those who do not help me."

It is not always necessary to say "Thank you" directly; sincere appreciation and praise can also convey gratitude. When we acknowledge someone's efforts, they feel valued and perform their tasks with greater joy and enthusiasm. This habit of expressing gratitude inspires us to embark on new paths and opens doors to possibilities we may not have imagined before.

Points for Contemplation:

- Have you ever participated in the chain of expressing gratitude?
- Have you expressed gratitude or praised anyone you encounter daily? Like sanitation workers, maids, postmen, etc.?
- After expressing gratitude to someone, notice the change in your feelings and also theirs. Does it motivate you and encourage them to do their best?

5

Associate Feeling with Gratitude

"No one who achieves success does so without acknowledging the help of others. The wise and confident acknowledge this help with gratitude."
- Alfred North Whitehead

When you read the line, "Thank you very much from the bottom of my heart," you might wonder what is being thanked. It is natural for everyone to assume there must be a reason behind expressing gratitude; why would someone thank without a reason?

We all experienced this as children. When guests came home with gifts, our parents instructed, "Say 'Thank you' to uncle and aunt." We often dutifully obliged and mechanically thanked them, eagerly anticipating the gift. If we were reluctant to thank them, perhaps out of sheer stubbornness, our mothers might warn, "No thank you, no chocolate." Sadly, sometimes, this warning proved true. To our young minds, it felt as if we would not receive the gift without saying "Thank you."

This is how many families teach manners to their children through a system of rewards and consequences. They teach them to say "Thank you" when someone gives them something. However, the children do not fully grasp the deeper meaning of "Thank you." They primarily learn to use it in certain situations. Teachers at school, parents at home, and older siblings instruct them on when and for what to say, "Thank you." As they grow up, they gradually understand they should say, "Thank you," not just when someone gives them something but also when someone helps them. Through this process, they learn the language of politeness.

Most people are familiar with common courtesies such as "Please," "Sorry," "Thank you," "Excuse me," and "You are welcome." While children may initially view these words as mere good manners, adults greatly benefit from their consistent use. By saying "Thank you," they enhance their communication skills, fostering more polite and cordial relationships while encouraging others to cooperate.

It is an excellent habit to say "Thank you" in daily conversations. However, the phrase "Thank you" holds much greater value than that. Despite its profound meaning, it has lost its significance today and has merely become a formality in modern communication and social etiquette. In essence, it has become transactional: "If you help me, I shall thank you. If I help you, you should thank me." This has diminished its genuine meaning, making it feel like a mechanical ritual.

It is as if you had Aladdin's magic lamp, with which you could have created great miracles, making your life better, happier, more creative, and prosperous. But instead of fully exploring its potential, you chose to use it only for transactional purposes, seeking cooperation from others and avoiding social disapproval. Some people even thank others for their selfish interests. They think, "If I thank the other person, they will comply with my requests or continue to support me."

Some people thank others so that they will be considered polite. But the true feeling of gratitude is much more than mere courtesy. It has the power to free us from the grip of despair, worry, negativity, sorrow, and feelings of lack, cultivating a sense of inner peace and serenity.

As children, we were taught to say, "Thank you," but rarely were we taught the underlying profoundness of this phrase. Understanding the true sentiments and the deeper significance of gratitude is crucial. We need to understand whether simply saying "Thank you" is enough or if there is something more significant to it.

Any word truly holds significance only when it is infused with genuine feeling. Without heartfelt feeling, it is just a hollow word devoid of value, not serving its intended purpose. Therefore, instead of mechanically uttering "Thank you," instill it with the genuine feeling of gratitude, appreciation, and heartfelt acknowledgment. Ramesh's story exemplifies this.

Ramesh grew up in a middle-class family. His father was an honest, hardworking, and dedicated teacher. From childhood, he instilled in Ramesh the values of hard work, honesty, and integrity. Every morning, he would take Ramesh to play football. He would personally tutor him in Mathematics and Science. With his father's firm support and guidance, Ramesh successfully completed his education and became a Chartered Accountant. Years later, when Ramesh became a director of a prestigious company, the first thing he did was make his father sit on his chair. He humbly touched his feet and said, "You are the rightful occupant of this seat because you made me capable of reaching this position. My heartfelt gratitude to you for bringing me to this stage."

To this day, Ramesh feels heartfelt gratitude for his father for every success he achieves. He often reminisces about his childhood, cherishing how his father instilled discipline and guided him at every step. He acknowledges that he could never have achieved this level of success without his father's support.

Whenever Ramesh feels, "Actually, this success is not mine alone; it belongs to my father," he wholeheartedly prays, "O God! Grant me the strength to always keep my father happy. May he live a healthy, joyful, and fulfilling life."

When you feel genuinely grateful for someone, you feel a powerful urge to do something for them. Even a small gift speaks volumes, revealing the sentiment behind it. A heartfelt blessing naturally emerges from within, shining with goodwill and warmth. This is the pure essence of gratitude.

Whenever we receive kindness, favor, or a helping hand, we should strive to cultivate the same feeling of gratitude as Ramesh and express our gratitude through meaningful actions or heartfelt words. When gratitude is expressed with genuine feeling, it touches the recipient's heart, and they also feel the love within us. Moreover, after sensing our love, their level of consciousness rises, making them feel good and deepening their bond with us.

In essence, the feeling behind gratitude makes us like a magnet. Even if we do not feel it genuinely at first, we can consciously act it out because this feeling creates space for abundance, positive thinking, and divine qualities to blossom within us. When we thank someone without genuine feelings, it is like one machine thanking another. It has no impact on the other person or us. In such a case, whether we thank the other person or not, it has no value. But when our gratitude is infused with genuine feeling, it touches the other person's soul, as though the Divine is expressing gratitude through us. This sincere expression of gratitude brings a smile to our faces, augments our happiness, and uplifts our spirits. This is the profound impact of genuine gratitude.

When we thank someone with a genuine feeling, our feeling touches them. When someone touches something with love and gives it to us, we should also accept it by touching it with love and then thank them. For example, if we receive money from someone, we should touch it with love and then thank them. This way, we associate the divine quality of genuine feeling with it. If you ever feel that you are not genuinely grateful, practice gratitude consciously, act it out, be happy, and see what happens.

If you want to thank someone, pause and reflect on the reason behind it. For example, if you wish to thank your parents, reflect on all they have done for you and then thank them. Begin by expressing heartfelt gratitude with at least one person in this way. Gradually, genuine gratitude will arise within you naturally.

Points for Contemplation:

- Do you say "Thank you" with genuine feeling, or is it merely a mechanical response?
- Make a list of five people to express your gratitude; reflect on all that they have done for you.
- Choose one person to express heartfelt gratitude; even if it is not a genuine feeling, act it out. Repeat this till a genuine feeling of gratitude awakens within you.

6

Freedom From a Life of Complaints

*"If a fellow isn't thankful for what he's got,
he isn't likely to be thankful for what he's going to get."*
- Frank A. Clark

When we are trapped by our comparing and judging minds, we often overlook our blessings and live lives filled with complaints. Like a tongue constantly aware of a missing tooth, we focus on what is lacking rather than appreciating what we have.

If we constantly dwell on negativity and find faults in everything, this negative mindset gradually erodes our strength and vitality. Complaining is a slow, bitter poison that mentally weakens us from within. It confines us to a narrow perspective, like a frog in a well, considering it to be their world, blind to the vast ocean of possibilities and beauty that exists beyond.

The habit of complaining compels us to curse life constantly. Some of the common complaints are: Why was it so hot yesterday? Why is it raining today? Why didn't they answer my call? Why did the other person speak sternly with me? Why did the meeting go on for so long? I had a late lunch. Why doesn't the maid come on time? She comes late and completes her work in haste. The train arrived late. The train was crowded. There is always a traffic jam. My wife came late from work and didn't cook my favorite dish for dinner. My son fared poorly in the exams; why can't he focus on his studies? I work so hard, but my salary is not enough. My husband is not spending enough time at home and so on. It is an endless list of complaints.

For most people, life has become like a bundle of complaints. Some even complain to God, "O God! How can You be so cruel? Why have You put me through so much suffering? What past-life sins am I paying for? I always think good of everyone, yet why do bad things always happen to me?"

Contemplate whether problems decrease or increase when you complain. Let us understand this through an old, well-known story where animals could speak.

> Once, in a barren desert, there lived a little bird perched upon a withered tree. She was often unwell, her feathers were thinning, and she had little to eat. Unable to fly in search of shelter or sustenance, she felt trapped. Day and night, she cursed her fate, plagued by the relentless desert heat. "O God," she cried, "Why have You abandoned me here in this forsaken place? Was this the best You could do for me? There is no water, no food, only this scorching sun. My feathers are falling, and I can't even fly to find a tree with shade." She spent her days steeped in misfortune and complaints.
>
> One day, a wandering hermit happened to pass by. Desperate for relief, the bird called out to him and asked, "O hermit, can you tell me when my suffering will end?" Moved by her plight, the hermit replied, "I can see into your past life, but not the future. Let me seek the wisdom of my guru and return with an answer for you."
>
> When the hermit met his guru, he recounted the bird's sorrowful tale. The guru listened thoughtfully, then said, "She must endure seven lifetimes of hardship, one suffering leading to the next." Deeply troubled, the hermit pleaded, "Is there no way for her to break free from this endless ordeal?" The guru paused, sat in silence for some time, and then replied, "There is a way. Tell her to chant a mantra continuously." Leaning in, he whispered the sacred words into the hermit's ear. When the hermit returned, he taught the bird the mantra, **"O God! Thank You for everything."** He instructed her to repeat it incessantly. With that, he left to return to his hermitage.
>
> Days later, while traveling through a lush, green forest, the hermit heard a beautiful melody. To his surprise, he spotted the very same bird once weighed down by despair, now singing joyfully. He was

The Miracle of Gratitude - 37

marveled at her transformation. She was vibrant and full of life, perched beside a shimmering pond, far from the barren desert.

The hermit, filled with wonder, rushed to his guru and asked, "Master, this bird was destined for seven lifetimes of suffering. How did this transformation happen so swiftly?" The guru smiled knowingly. "When you gave her the mantra, she was skeptical. She began chanting it half-heartedly, treating it like a mere ritual. Soon after you left, she collapsed on the scorching desert sand, thirsty and exhausted. For the first time, instead of lamenting, she whispered sincerely, '**O God! Thank You for everything. I am thirsty and unable to fly, but perhaps there is a purpose even in this. For this, I am deeply grateful.**'

"For the first time, instead of succumbing to despair and complaining, she chose a new response. Deep down, she felt that something better would happen with this. This shift in mindset brought her slight relief from her pain and mustered up some courage. Coincidentally, a compassionate bird lover traveling from one city to another passed by. He noticed her plight, gave her water, and gently carried her to the pond.

"From that day on, whenever she encountered problems, she thanked God instead of feeling sad. With each expression of gratitude, her suffering eased, and the pain destined for her seven lifetimes vanished within a few days. Gradually, she became completely healthy."

Expressing gratitude for everything changes our circumstances. It shifts our mindset from negativity to positivity, opening us to abundance. If you want to change your life, start thanking God for everything. Miracles can unfold in your life, too! Instead of complaining, embrace every situation with gratitude.

If you fall, be thankful. If you miss out on your favorite meal, be grateful. If there isn't enough salt in your food, be thankful. If someone bumps into you, doesn't pick up your call, doesn't reply to your message, or doesn't "like" your social media post, still thank them. If a family member makes you late for work, instead of complaining, go to work with a grateful heart. If your boss scolds you, silently thank them. Initially, you may need to give a logical reason to your mind, "My boss is scolding me for my own good. If my expertise improves, I will only grow. Therefore, thanks to my boss." With practice, you will get so habituated to be thankful that you won't need a reason to thank. Gratitude will become your second nature. You will thank God for everything.

When you start living with gratitude, you will find complaints gradually diminishing. Eventually, you will begin to lead a complaint-free life.

The vicious cycle of complaints and lack

Complaints stem from a feeling of lack, and each complaint only intensifies this feeling. Gratitude is the only way to break free of this vicious cycle. Express gratitude for everything.

Have you ever felt genuinely grateful for something while also complaining about it? Probably not! Our minds can hold either gratitude or complaints about someone. Both cannot coexist at the same time. They are mutually exclusive. Therefore, start thanking the very things you complain about. Even if your mind resists, deeming it illogical, take a small step toward it. Shift your perspective.

Just like the bird who reluctantly thanked at first but ultimately regained the strength to fly in the sky, we, too, will feel happy and liberated by simply expressing gratitude.

In moments of unawareness, some people complain to their parents, "What have you done for us? You did not give us a good upbringing, time, or affection." In contrast, others thank their parents, "You gave us a good education. You raised us amidst your own struggles and empowered us to stand on our own feet. We are eternally grateful for this." They understand that their parents gave them the best they could.

When we honor and thank our parents, we model that behavior for our children. When we express heartfelt gratitude to our parents and understand their feelings, our family bond becomes stronger.

Points for Contemplation:

- How often do you complain? Make a list of five complaints and reframe them with gratitude: "O God, thank you for ……(complaint)"
- Where does your focus reside—on lack or abundance?
- Are you grateful for your parents? Express it to them verbally or in writing. If you have children, involve them in expressing gratitude to their grandparents.

7

Wearing the Cloak of Gratitude

*"If Compassion is a form of love,
Gratitude is its evolved form."*
- **Sirshree**

To comprehend the depth of gratitude, let us delve deeper into the feeling of thankfulness. Let us understand how this feeling changes our mental state and permeates our entire being.

Saint Meera, renowned for her ardent devotion to Lord Krishna, epitomizes divine devotion. At the tender age of three, she traveled with her grandfather. When they stopped over at a camp, they met a monk. The monk possessed a small idol of Lord Krishna, which captivated little Meera at first sight. Lost in adoration, she fervently pleaded for the idol.

The monk, who considered the idol his personal deity, respectfully declined her request, bound by tradition. Her grandfather gently tried to reason with her, promising to get a similar idol later. However, little Meera insisted on having that very idol and even refused to eat food that day.

That night, Lord Krishna appeared in the monk's dream and inquired, "If you cannot part with my idol, how will you share my devotion with others? Your purpose is to spread devotion to all."

Deeply moved by this divine message, the monk presented his cherished idol to Meera the very next morning. Overjoyed, she embraced it, her heart overflowing with gratitude and devotion.

This story exemplifies how Meera's unwavering devotion and fasting blossomed into a cherished blessing. In the end, she received her beloved Lord Krishna's idol. Later in life, as she matured, her boundless gratitude led her to find Lord Krishna within her heart.

Few people genuinely grasp the true spirit of gratitude and its transformative impact. Consequently, many often mistakenly express gratitude only after their prayers are answered or their wishes are fulfilled. But the fundamental essence of gratitude is immersing yourself in this sublime feeling even before receiving anything, just as little Meera did. Embrace heartfelt gratitude from this very moment. Do not wait until you receive something. This aligns you fully with the feeling of gratitude.

Upon seeing the idol, little Meera was overwhelmed with profound devotion and gratitude. Even when she didn't get the idol, she observed a fast and immersed herself in the remembrance of Lord Krishna. Her unwavering devotion ultimately paved the way for the idol to enter her life.

Just as we adapt our clothing to protect ourselves from every season, like cozy shawls in the chill of winter, raincoats in the downpour of the rainy season, and sun coats, caps in the summer heat, we should also wrap ourselves in the cloak of gratitude to protect us from life's challenges. Immersing ourselves in the heartfelt feeling of gratitude is a unique cloak that can be always worn, even until the last moment of life. Its exceptional beauty lies in the fact that it is a priceless gift that costs us absolutely nothing.

If we could truly comprehend the experiences of great souls and saints who have embraced gratitude, we would begin to grasp its extraordinary, life-transforming power. Even today, countless individuals are embracing this sacred feeling. By cultivating gratitude, we, too, can unlock its grandeur and achieve miraculous results, just as Saint Meera did.

When we infuse prayers with gratitude, we become like magnets, attracting all positivity into our lives. This feeling embodies all divine qualities, acting as a powerful force that strengthens our connection to the Universe's abundant blessings.

The above story of Saint Meera is not merely a tale to be heard and forgotten. It is a profound lesson that must be deeply ingrained in our lives. We can cultivate a daily practice of embracing gratitude, much like donning a protective cloak. Imagine starting each day enveloped in this feeling of thankfulness. How would your day unfold? How would it transform your routine and, ultimately, your entire life?

The key lesson from Saint Meera's story is that **even in the toughest situations, prayer is always possible.** In the Indian epic Ramayana, Mother Sita constantly prayed during her captivity in the Ashoka Vatika. The strength she gained from this prayer empowered Lord Rama and his allies to build the Ram Setu bridge to cross the sea, and reach Lanka, eventually leading to her rescue.

There is a well-known saying in the Bible: "To the one who has, more will be given, and he will have an abundance, but from the one who has not, even what he has will be taken away." This principle suggests that the "Yes, I have" feeling turns us into a powerful magnet, attracting all good things in life. Gratitude nurtures and strengthens this feeling. If we live in gratitude, the feeling of abundance will increase, while in its absence, even what little remains will also fade away. Keeping this in mind, reflect on your life; whatever prosperity, harmonious relationships, and health you have, wrap yourself in the cloak of gratitude, and be thankful for all these blessings.

Gratitude Meditation

This meditation will help you experience a profound feeling of gratitude. First, carefully read and understand the instructions thoroughly before practicing them. You may choose to record them in your voice and listen later. Just as Saint Meera immersed herself in devotion, let us now immerse ourselves fully in gratitude.

Find a serene place where you can gently turn in circles. Set a timer for 10 minutes. Embodying the spirit of a Sufi saint and emulating Saint Meera's state of divine devotion, practice this meditation to fully immerse yourself in gratitude. Be open to every blessing life offers, trusting that it is part of a divine plan.

Embrace the feeling of "Thy will is my will," and be open to the blessings showered on you.

Imagine a divine white light enveloping you.

Bathed in this divine grace, feel all impurities dissolve and vices getting eradicated. You are transcending the limitations of Passivity, Hyperactivity, and Equanimity and merging with a state of pure awareness.

Slowly start turning around, as if gathering divine blessings with each gentle spin.

Engage in this prayerful motion not merely with closed eyes but with the intention of allowing the power of gratitude to permeate your entire being.

If your feeling of gratitude wanes, immediately chant, "Thank you" to regain your grateful state.

Whenever confronted with negativity in life, recall these moments of deep gratitude. Visualize the feeling of gratitude descending upon you, completely cloaking you. Feel grateful for the countless blessings and abundance that grace your life.

Continue turning comfortably as long as it feels natural. When the time is up, gently pause and sit down. Rest in silence for a few moments, then, slowly open your eyes.

With consistent practice, you will feel so deeply rooted in this state of devotion that you can reconnect to it whenever you wish.

Points for Contemplation:

- What did you learn from Meera's story?
- Do you start each day with thankfulness? How does that transform your day, routine, and life?
- How do you feel after the gratitude meditation?

8

Perceiving Virtues with Gratitude

"Gratitude is one of the most profound lessons of life, which when learnt, fills our life with love, joy, and peace."
- Sirshree

There is an inherent ego functioning within each person, leading them to feel, "I am separate," "I am different from others," and "I am better." They consider themselves superior and belittle others. Consequently, they become habitual in criticizing others. When they see others succeed or possess good qualities, they develop jealousy and hatred toward them, preventing them from feeling grateful. These tendencies hinder their ability to always remain in gratitude. As long as they are unaware of this truth and remain trapped in the web of comparison and judgment, how can gratitude emerge within them? Believing themselves to be superior to others itself means they are behind them. Let us understand this with an example.

Imagine each of us wearing two-locket necklaces with one locket in the front and the other on the back. Our positive qualities are written on the front locket, while our weaknesses are written on the back locket. All of this is in the unseen. When we perceive flaws in others, it means we are behind them, focusing on the flaws written on their back locket. Thus, we are behind all the people in whom we see faults. Conversely, we are ahead of all the people in whom we see good qualities.

By constantly dwelling on others' mistakes, we regress. As a result, we attract negativity, problems, and difficulties into our lives. We start facing issues in various areas, including finances, health, and relationships. When this happens, we often complain, "O God! Why does this happen to me alone?" If God were to answer, He might say, **"Whatever you focus on will manifest within you, and whatever you reflect upon is what you will become."**

Now, pause for a moment and reflect, "What have I truly achieved in my life so far?" Write down your five core positive qualities and five prominent flaws in a journal. Contemplate how you acquired the positive qualities, like reading informative books, respecting others, or being patient. At some point of time, you must have appreciated them, pondered over them, and understood their significance. On the contrary, the flaws you see in yourself, were also unknowingly observed in others. This aligns with the Law of Nature: **Whatever you focus on multiplies in your life.** When you focus on negativity, it manifests in your life; when you focus on positivity, you attract that, too.

Having understood this, how should you choose to live? Should you let things continue as they are, or should you actively strive for change? If you continue doing what you have always done, you will keep reaping the same results. Therefore, resolve right now: From today, only positive things will come into my life. I will consciously focus only on good qualities in people, even if my mind resists. This may seem challenging at first, but with consistent practice, you can master it, and it will become your second nature.

You can make use of the following three steps to cultivate gratitude within yourself:

1. Repeat positive affirmations

- I will consciously see, think, and speak only positive things.
- I expect miracles every day. I am getting better in all five aspects of life: Physical, mental, financial, social, and spiritual.
- I am living a life of purity and righteousness, surrounded by only well-wishers.
- Everyone around me is kind and supportive.

2. Make a resolution

- Resolve to refrain from watching bad news on TV and reading about bloodshed and violence because what you see influences your thoughts, and your emotions are formed accordingly.

- Resolve to choose a worthy person as your role model. We closely observe our role model and attract their qualities into our lives. Yet, often unknowingly, we are swayed by the external appearance and fleeting triumphs of others, mistaking them as our role models. However, our role model should be someone who is truly happy and lives a virtuous life.

  Reflect, "Who is that person in my life whom I know closely, and who exemplifies an ideal life?" This could be your teacher, principal, doctor, guru, philanthropist, or someone who lives a happy, healthy, and selfless life. Seeing them, you should pray, "May my life mirror theirs. I aspire to live my life like them."

  Now, write down the five most admirable qualities of that role model in your journal. Close your eyes and envision yourself embracing these virtues. Resolve in your mind to call or meet your role model and tell them, "I admire these qualities in you, and I am imbibing them within myself."

3. Accept the 21-day challenge

In this challenge, identify one positive quality in at least one person each day. Share it with them and write it down in your journal every day for 21 days so that by the end of these 21 days, these qualities will take root in your mind and DNA. You can adopt some creative ways to do this.

- When wishing friends and loved ones on their birthdays or anniversaries, make a conscious effort to highlight a specific quality you admire in them, so that they feel encouraged, and you internalize that quality within yourself. Seek out people who embody the qualities you wish to cultivate within yourself and sincerely appreciate them for the same.

  For instance, a financially successful person might exude the qualities of abundance and generosity. They might possess the art of ethically earning and accumulating wealth in a disciplined manner. Similarly, a physically fit person embodies healthy habits to maintain their overall well-being. Surround yourself with such people whose qualities you wish to embrace. Appreciate them and express gratitude for these virtues so that your life is also filled with miracles.

- When you meet people, smile and acknowledge one of their positive qualities. If you cannot share it directly, verbalize it silently in your mind. Through this practice, you welcome them into your life, and they will soon become a part of your life. Begin with your family and people around you—your family members, neighbors, colleagues, and even those who enrich your daily existence by providing everyday services like the security guard, cleaner, office assistant, etc.
- Select 21 people from your contacts list and send them a message appreciating an admirable quality they possess.

These practices can help you cultivate a deeper sense of gratitude in your life.

Points for Contemplation:

- What do you usually see in other people—their qualities or shortcomings?
- Which qualities do you want to imbibe? Make a list of these qualities and find out if anyone close to you has these qualities.
- Are you ready for the 21-day challenge? Write your experience at the end of the challenge in your journal.

PART 2

The Glory of Gratitude and its Practice

9

The Science of Gratitude

"Gratitude makes sense of our past, brings peace for today, and creates a vision for tomorrow."
- Melody Beattie

Research was conducted to explore the impact of gratitude on individuals seeking counseling for stress and depression. Participants were randomly divided into two groups. The first group, consisting of 22 participants was given a brief exercise. Before each counseling session, they were instructed to spend 20 minutes writing a gratitude letter. This involved thanking all the positive experiences in their lives, the people who supported them, and their loved ones. The second group, however, was not given this exercise.

Six months later, their MRI scans revealed a significant difference. For those in the first group, who had practiced gratitude journaling, the part of the brain associated with positive emotions exhibited increased activity. They reported heightened levels of happiness and positivity while experiencing a concurrent decrease in negative emotions such as despair and regret.

Many psychologists have discovered through their research that cultivating gratitude can significantly shift negative thought patterns toward more positive ones.

When we feel grateful, it activates the medial prefrontal cortex, a region of our brain that experiences happiness and controls our emotions. This activation alleviates pain and distress, regulates heart rate, and prevents depression. Consequently, the calmer mind fosters many positive effects on the body, including improved sleep quality, increased energy levels, an uplifted mood, and a strengthened immune system. These benefits ultimately lead to a more fulfilling and enthusiastic life.

Research indicates that when one dwells in the feeling of gratitude, their brains become more capable of expressing it. Once they cultivate the habit of expressing gratitude, even for seemingly trivial things, this habit becomes more deeply ingrained. This consistent practice fosters joy and fulfillment, highlighting the profound impact of gratitude.

There is a popular story of the Buddha dating back to the period when his monastic order, the *Sangha*, was growing significantly. Many individuals were drawn to his teachings and joined the Sangha. During this period, the province of Suna was infamous for its brutality, where people would kill each other even for minor transgressions.

One day, the Buddha addressed his disciples, "We must journey to this province to spread our message and awaken the people over there. Who among you is willing to undertake this challenging mission?"

A hush fell over the assembly as the Buddha's question hung in the air. None of the monks dared to venture into such a perilous journey. However, a young monk, who was not very well-educated, stepped forward to accept this daunting task.

The Buddha gently inquired, "It is good that you are willing to go, but what will you do if the people there treat you rudely?"

The monk, eyes shining with unwavering resolve, replied, "O Enlightened One! I will be grateful that they only treated me rudely but did not dishonor me."

The Buddha continued, "Good! But what if they resort to violence and beat you?"

The monk, in a firm voice, answered, "I will thank them for beating me but not killing me."

"And what if they choose to end your life?" the Buddha pressed.

"Then I will die thanking them wholeheartedly for being the cause of my liberation," the monk replied with unwavering calm.

"You are indeed prepared and worthy to complete this noble mission. You may go," the Buddha declared.

The monk in the story exemplifies the profound power of gratitude. By cultivating gratitude even in the most challenging circumstances, he transcended fear and embraced a higher purpose. This perspective is a gift of gratitude. If we feel grateful for all the incidents in life, both good and bad, our lives can become simple, straightforward, and powerful, just like that of the monk. Gratitude is indeed an important pillar of our lives.

Let us delve deeper into how gratitude works.

There are intricate neural pathways in our brains that facilitate the transmission of information. These pathways are created by the way we interact with people and react to situations in life. Over time, these pathways become well-established, serving as easy and default routes for our subconscious mind to follow. Consequently, when faced with similar situations, we often react in the same way.

You may have noticed that when commuting to work or running market errands, you consistently choose the familiar route, even if alternative options exist. This tendency reflects how deeply ingrained neural pathways, consciously or unconsciously, influence our decision-making.

You may have likely experienced situations when someone raises their voice, and you respond in the same manner impulsively. While you could have chosen to stay calm, the tendency to react is so ingrained in your neural pathways that you are unconsciously driven to do so.

Thus, neural pathways are formed in our brains for every situation we encounter. Deep-rooted through repetition, these pathways become habitual and guide our subconscious mind to follow them like an obedient servant. Consequently, when faced with similar situations, we tend to elicit predictable emotional responses and subsequent behaviors.

You may have observed people reacting differently to heavy rains. Some feel refreshed and joyful, appreciating the lush greenery that follows. However, others may feel disappointed, focusing on the resulting mud and dirt. This disparity in response stems from the fact that our brains are programmed by our experiences and beliefs since childhood, leading us to perceive and react to the same event in completely different ways.

Now, if you were asked, "Would you like to change your old programming to alter the ingrained neural pathways that limit you?" your response would undoubtedly be a resounding, "Yes!" But naturally, the next question would arise, "How can I achieve this? What do I need to do?"

When you begin expressing gratitude for what you already have, your thought patterns and the programming of your subconscious mind will begin to change. It will rewire the existing pathways, gradually replacing them with new ones through repetition. This shift in perspective can unlock the inherent grace and beauty that life offers.

You may have encountered people with diverse temperaments—some perpetually cheerful, while others perpetually stressed. Some overthink minor issues, while others dwell on endless complaints. But the good news is that it is never too late to make a positive change. You can eliminate your wrong tendencies by cultivating a mindset of gratitude and consciously redirecting your thoughts.

When you start expressing gratitude consistently, it gradually weakens the ingrained neural pathways associated with negative emotions while simultaneously strengthening those associated with positive emotions. This transformation enables you to navigate life with a renewed perspective.

A unique way to bring positive thoughts

Our mind constantly engages in self-talk, commenting on whatever is happening around us. This internal dialogue shapes our thought patterns and personality. The state of our mind directly influences how we perceive situations, ultimately determining whether we experience fear, weakness, strength, or inner peace.

Recognizing the profound influence of our thoughts on our lives, we can consciously guide them in a positive direction to create a favorable internal environment that supports our overall well-being.

A simple yet powerful way to cultivate positive thoughts is to dwell in the feeling of gratitude. When we appreciate the blessings bestowed on us by Nature, it becomes easier to let go of negative and futile thoughts.

You may have likely observed that whenever something good or bad happens, the mind tends to gravitate more toward the negative than the positive. Even amidst abundant joyful memories, the mind often highlights the unfavorable aspects of life. To counter this inherent bias, we must constantly practice bringing ourselves into a feeling of gratitude.

When you find yourself overwhelmed by negative thoughts or stress, consciously remind yourself, "Now, I must shift my focus to the blessings I have received. I must recall the things that bring me joy." There must have been at least one experience during the day that brought you happiness. Embrace that.

In this way, by consistently expressing gratitude, your thought patterns will shift in a new direction, and your perspective toward situations will also change. When faced with challenging situations in the future, you will be better equipped to navigate them peacefully or learn the skill to handle them effectively.

As our feelings are, so are our thoughts. When we consciously focus on our blessings, our thought patterns begin to change. By simply being in a state of gratitude, we can effectively eliminate many negative tendencies within ourselves.

Points for Contemplation:

- What did you learn from the story of the Buddha? How will you apply it into your life?
- List five troublesome situations where you would like to change your thought patterns by expressing gratitude.
- How will you change your self-talk in stressful situations to bring positivity?

10

The Importance of Gratitude in Action

"The root of joy is gratefulness. It is not joy that makes us grateful; it is gratitude that makes us joyful."
- David Steindl-Rast

One day, a student went to his teacher's house to meet him after the academic year. He had topped the exams and was eager to thank the teacher. He found his teacher deeply engrossed in his writing despite a power outage and the scorching heat. He quietly waited in a corner for the teacher to finish. Just then, the teacher received a phone call and got busy with the conversation. When he finished the call, he noticed the student and enquired about his visit. The student replied, "I have come to express my gratitude for your guidance. I achieved top marks in the exams."

At that very moment, the power returned, the fan whirred to life and spun rapidly. The teacher's papers got scattered all over the place. The student calmly watched the teacher meticulously gathering the papers. Once the papers were neatly stacked, the teacher resumed his seat. The student then stepped forward, bowed respectfully, and expressed his gratitude before leaving. The teacher, undisturbed, resumed his work.

While the student genuinely felt grateful to his teacher, was it enough to simply bow and verbally express gratitude? Although he verbally thanked the teacher, he could have demonstrated more meaningful gratitude by helping the teacher—he could have readily offered to gather the scattered papers.

The point is that gratitude can be expressed not only through words but also through meaningful actions. When you assist someone out of gratitude, it fosters a more profound sense of peace and contentment.

Expressing gratitude through action

Imagine someone saying, "I am grateful for the beauty of nature." Yet when they go on a picnic, they litter indiscriminately, damage plants, and disrupt the eco-balance by carelessly throwing plastic bags around. Is this a genuine expression of gratitude? No, it is merely a fleeting expression devoid of any genuine action.

While expressing gratitude through words is essential, it alone does not suffice. For instance, thanking God daily for a healthy body is a commendable start, but genuine gratitude requires action. We must manifest our gratitude by maintaining a balanced diet and engaging in regular exercise.

When we express gratitude in advance for something we desire, the Universe conspires to bring it to us. Even when doubts arise, our heartfelt gratitude serves as faith in action, increasing the likelihood of our desires manifesting.

For example, if you dream of buying a house, purchase a carpet for your new home in advance and thank the Universe for it. If you aspire to buy a car, buy a keychain as your faith-in-action. If you anticipate financial abundance, keep some money in your wallet as a welcoming gesture for prosperity. Alternatively, you can take your family on a special outing or donate to charity as an expression of your gratitude for impending blessings. This is faith-in-action, which draws the desired things toward you each day.

Creative ways to express gratitude

Gauri, a third-year student in Commercial Art, was dealing with a challenging project topic as part of her syllabus. Her friend Minakshi provided invaluable assistance in successfully completing the project.

External examiners arrived to assess the projects and Gauri's project was awarded second place. While Gauri's dedication and hard work undoubtedly contributed to her success, Minakshi's support played a crucial role.

Deeply grateful for Minakshi's invaluable help, Gauri wanted to express her sincere appreciation and gratitude in a meaningful way. She knew Minakshi loved *Gajar ka Halwa* (An Indian sweet), so she prepared it herself and treated Minakshi. Through this simple yet thoughtful gesture, Gauri expressed her heartfelt gratitude in a creative and meaningful way.

Offering a cherished gift to someone who has helped us can be a beautiful way to express our gratitude. Similarly, when we appreciate someone's qualities, it is yet another form of saying thank you. Let us understand this with another example.

One morning, Mahesh's boss summoned him into his office with an exciting news: "The car model you designed has been selected!" Later, during a team meeting, the boss publicly praised Mahesh, saying, "Mahesh, I deeply admire your dedication and commitment. I am incredibly proud to have a colleague like you." By acknowledging Mahesh's hard work and commitment in front of the team, the boss innovatively expressed his gratitude in a meaningful and impactful way.

Let us consider one more example.

John Kralik, a 52-year-old honest lawyer, was grappling a significant downturn in his personal and professional life. Day by day, his situation seemed to deteriorate. One day, he went hiking deep into the forest to seek solace. As he quietly sat on a rock, he pondered, "Why am I so unhappy, troubled, and overwhelmed by my circumstances?"

Suddenly, an inner voice resonated, "If you do not feel grateful for what you have, you will remain perpetually troubled."

He sat in silence, contemplating these words of wisdom. With newfound clarity, he resolved, "From today, I will write a thank-you note every day. I will express gratitude for whatever I have." Immediately, he felt a surge of energy and renewed hope.

He began writing a heartfelt thank-you note to his elder son: "Thank you so much for being in my life."

This simple act of gratitude worked like a miracle. The very next day, his son unexpectedly visited him and returned the borrowed money with a sincere apology for the delay. John was astonished, as he had almost forgotten about the transaction. It felt like a beautiful dream, and he was filled with an overwhelming sense of joy.

The following day, John penned a heartfelt thank-you note to his younger son, who, as if by serendipity, visited him. Inspired by this experience, John resolved to write thank-you notes to everyone who had helped him in his life, including opponents, lawyers, brokers, friends, and employees. He diligently wrote one thank-you note every day. Now, he had a newfound purpose and a reason to live each day. His loneliness began to fade away, and he started feeling enthusiastic and energized.

Over the course of six months, he diligently composed nearly one hundred and eighty thank-you notes. This daily practice of gratitude profoundly transformed his life. His financial and social standing gradually improved, fostering renewed connection with others, opening doors to new work opportunities, and he experienced steady progress in his legal career. Eventually, he achieved remarkable success as a judge in California.

You, too, can embark on a similar experiment and witness the transformative power of gratitude. If you hesitate to thank someone directly, consider composing a heartfelt thank-you note just as John did. If you post the note, that's wonderful. Even if you don't post it, as you pen the thank-you note to the other person, your genuine feelings are subtly conveyed to their subconscious mind. As a result, your relationship with them will improve significantly.

Points for Contemplation:

- What is the difference between expressing gratitude in words and in action?
- If you want to manifest something in your life, like a car or house, how will you put faith into action?
- Write a thank-you note for everyone in your family and friends, and then extend it to everyone who has helped you in your life. Observe how it is changing your life and bringing happiness and well-being.

11

Thanking The Three Aspects of God

*"In gratitude, nothing is lost, but much is gained.
In complaints, nothing is gained, but much is lost."*
- Anonymous

When we make a purchase at a shop, we always collect a receipt after paying the bill. Similarly, when we deposit money in a bank, we always ensure to collect a receipt. Even with online transactions, we deem a payment as complete only when we receive a confirmation message. The receipt or confirmation serves as an irrefutable proof that our transaction is complete.

Similarly, when someone puts in effort for our sake, and we acknowledge their work, express sincere gratitude, and appreciate the significance of their invaluable support, we are, in essence, giving them a mental receipt of thanks.

Today, let us attain completeness toward God, the Supreme Power, with our deepest gratitude, not just to one, but three Gods. First, we express thanks to the Universal Supreme Being. Next, we offer gratitude to the divine presence in others. Finally, we thank the divine presence within ourselves, the sacred spark of life within us.

Let us explore each of these.

The First God - the Supreme Being

The first aspect of God is the Origin and omniscient essence of all creation—the Sustainer of life, the Supreme Providence whose presence upholds the universe. This Divine Source is revered by myriad names, including Lord Rama, Lord Krishna, Allah, and Christ.

Across all faiths, people recognize a Supreme Power that sustains and guides the universe in perfect harmony. This is the Supreme Consciousness we revere and thank for orchestrating the vastness of creation. Nature's grand symphony unfolds with awe-inspiring precision, where everything happens spontaneously in a self-organized balance. Every prayer finds its answer. Let us delve into a small story to grasp the beauty of this wondrous design.

> A couple dreams of providing their child with the finest education, hoping he will flourish and become successful. Though their financial means are modest, they long to enroll him in a prestigious university. The father contemplates switching to a more lucrative job to ease the burden of supporting his son's education. Meanwhile,

The Miracle of Gratitude - 65

the child, too, dreams of studying abroad and earnestly prays for this opportunity to unfold. They both were praying for their wishes to be fulfilled.

Then, the miracle of Nature unfolds in the most unexpected way. The child is granted the chance to study abroad, but how? The father is offered a job overseas—an opportunity beyond their wildest dreams. Nature wove the family's prayers into a seamless and harmonious tapestry, manifesting this perfect arrangement that not only fulfilled their wishes but also kept them united in a foreign land.

We should be deeply grateful for this beautiful orchestration by God. Nature provides for every living being according to their needs and disposition. This is the miracle of gratitude for Nature's divine order. In perfect timing, all that we need gracefully finds its way to us, without fail.

Everything unfolds in the presence of God, and God never makes mistakes. Each event, each moment, is a thread in the grand divine plan crafted for our highest evolution. When we cultivate unwavering faith in this truth, we embody gratitude toward the Supreme Providence. Whether it is summer, winter, or the monsoons, let us thank God for every season. Our trust, love, and devotion to this Supreme Presence fill us with a profound sense of gratitude.

The Second God - the Divine in others

The second aspect of God is, recognizing the divine presence within every being. Each individual is a reflection of God, embodying that sacred essence. They serve as mirrors for us, and when we express gratitude from this perspective, we can navigate even the most challenging interactions or situations. Regardless of whether someone plays a positive or negative role in our lives, gratitude can emerge within us for them. By honoring the divine presence in our relatives, friends, colleagues, neighbors, loved ones, and even competitors, we can accept their behavior with grace. Instead of nurturing resentment, we can chose to be grateful by understanding that they are catalysts guiding us toward our highest evolution.

The Third God - the Divine within us

The third aspect of God is the divine presence within us. Just as God holds goodwill for all beings, our Divine Self, desires only goodness for all. Recognizing this truth fills us with gratitude for the divine presence within. Instead of condemning ourselves, we learn to love ourselves. So, whenever feelings of guilt, insecurity, lack, or helplessness arise, we offer gratitude to our Divine Self and affirm, "I am one with God, and I have the strength to release these negative emotions. I deeply love myself, and I am letting go of all that does not align with my true nature."

When we recognize God within ourselves, honor the Divine in others, and sense the divine presence around us, we enter a state of knowing where nothing remains hidden. In this elevated awareness, we bask in gratitude for God, who enlivens our body and mind. Every aspect of our lives—physical, mental, social, financial, and spiritual—is elevated to new heights. Bathed in the shower of gratitude, every action is imbued with this profound sense of thankfulness.

This world is a grand exhibition where Nature presents a vast array of experiences. Some stalls in this cosmic exhibition offer material attractions and tempting illusions, while others remind us of the presence of God. As we navigate through life's exhibition, encountering both right and wrong, truth and falsehood, good and bad, if we observe it all with detachment, we remain anchored in unwavering gratitude. This profound understanding—that "I am one with God, and all others are also one with God"—keeps us deeply connected to the divine presence.

Starting today, let us consciously express gratitude to all three aspects of God. Express your gratitude aloud, feel it deeply within your heart, reflect on it in your thoughts, and embody it in your actions—this is the true essence of gratitude. Such a practice guides us toward wholeness and fulfillment, drawing us closer to the divine presence in all creation.

Here is a simple prayer to honor these three aspects of God. First read it. Then, with closed eyes, either silently or aloud, repeat it.

"O Supreme God!

Everything unfolds and flows in your sacred presence.

Thank you for being the Supreme Providence

that guides and nurtures me.

Thank you for your divine presence in others,

reflecting your sacred essence in every situation.

Thank you for your presence within me,

guiding me with love toward my highest evolution.

For your presence, for your grace,

Thank you, Thank you, Thank you..."

Points for Contemplation:

- Express gratitude for the Supreme Being.
- Express gratitude for the Divine in others.
- Express gratitude for the Divine within us.

12

Embrace the Abundance of Nature

"Those who possess the ability to express gratitude are always contented."
- **Anonymous**

Have you ever seen Nature expressing sadness? Never! Birds keep chirping, their joyful melodies uplifting us and drawing us into their world, even if only for a few moments. When we step outside for an early morning walk, the trees along the path, laden with blossoms which are a kaleidoscope of colors and fragrances, invigorate our spirits and fill us with freshness and enthusiasm for the day ahead.

Nature's beauty radiates through trees, gardens, flowers, rivers, waterfalls, oceans, mountains, and animals, all teeming with love and joy. Everywhere we look, we see a constant stream of pure love.

All living beings in nature are bound by invisible laws. Acceptance and free flow are the Laws of Nature. Where there is ease, joy, and harmony, there can be no space for hatred or struggle. All beings thrive in this interconnected tapestry, weaving sweet bonds and flourishing in this harmonious symphony of existence.

If we look within ourselves, do we readily accept everything? Does our mental state allow us to flow naturally through life, unburdened by stress?

Often, we feel burdened by sorrow or physical discomfort. Sometimes, we become overwhelmed by feeling of lack or dissatisfaction when we look at

others and compare. At times, even the most trivial inconveniences trigger a cascade of complaints within us.

Can we truly enjoy Nature's bounty in such a state of inner resistance? No! Living in sorrow or frustration drifts us away from Nature's rhythm, leaving us in a vicious cycle of worry and distress. How can we develop the ability to live free from anxiety and tension and embrace Nature's blessings?

When we express heartfelt gratitude to God for the blessings in our lives, to those around us, and dwell in the spirit of thankfulness, our inner state begins to change, gradually dissolving the negativity within us. Consequently, we begin to feel God's loving presence. Love, joy, and peace start flowing toward us from all directions, connecting us to the supreme consciousness that powers the entire creation.

By living in the spirit of gratitude, we become positive magnets, attracting the highest and best the Universe offers. This continuous flow of positivity purifies our minds and hearts, dispelling negativity and aligning us more closely with the harmonious rhythm of Nature. In this rhythm, we draw only joy and goodness into our lives.

Whenever faced with negativity, our level of awareness drops first. Actions taken from this state of lowered awareness are rarely successful, often leading to clouded decisions and ineffective responses, which can even worsen our circumstances.

> A man had been burdened by stress and worry for many months, which left him feeling irritable and constantly on edge. He was distressed by the weight of bearing all the household expenses, shouldering the full responsibility for his entire family. To complicate the matter further, various friends and relatives frequently visited, magnifying his sense of burden.
>
> This ongoing tension caused him to scold his children often and have frequent arguments with his wife. One day, his son approached him, inquiring, "Dad, can you please help me with my homework?" Already stressed, the father angrily sent his son away. Later, after his temper had cooled, the father went to check on him. He found his son fast asleep, his homework notebook still clutched in his hand. As the father gently tried to set the notebook down, his eyes fell on

the title of his son's assignment: "Write a thank-you note for things that don't seem good at first but turn out to be good later."

The child's assignment required him to write a passage on this topic, which he had completed. Driven by curiosity, the father started to read. The child wrote:

"I am very grateful for my annual exams. They seem awful at first, but they always bring much anticipated school vacations afterward."

"I am thankful for bitter medicines, which taste unpleasant at first but help me get well."

"I am so thankful for the alarm clock that wakes me every morning. It makes me grumpy but ensures I always wake up on time."

"I am deeply grateful for having such a loving father. His scoldings can sometimes feel harsh, but he buys me toys, takes me out, gives me delicious food, and showers love on us. I feel lucky to have a father, especially since my friend Soham doesn't have one."

Reading his son's homework, the father felt as if he had been suddenly awakened from a slumber; his perspective shifted dramatically. The child's gratitude resonated in his mind, especially the part about him as a father. Sleep eluded him that night as he sat in silence, reflecting on his worries with a newfound, fresh perspective:

"I bear all the household expenses, which means I have a home! By God's grace, I am fortunate compared to those without a roof or enduring the uncertainty of living in rented homes with no place to truly call their own"

"I carry the responsibility for my family, which means I have a family—a loving wife and adorable children. I am blessed compared to those who walk this world alone."

"Friends and relatives frequently visit me, which means I am surrounded by loved ones who enrich my life and with whom I can share my joys and woes."

"O God! Thank you deeply. Forgive me for not seeing the countless blessings that have graced my life."

The Miracle of Gratitude

After this, the father's perspective took a complete U-turn. All his worries and anxieties vanished as if they had never existed. He awakened to a profound new understanding. Rushing to his son's bedside, he gently lifted the sleeping child into his arms, kissed his forehead, and caressed him with tear-filled eyes. He poured out

his gratitude to his son and God. A profound peace settled over him as he drifted to sleep with a beautiful realization—he was not just cradling his child; he was himself being nestled in the loving embrace of God.

This poignant story reveals how stress and distorted thinking can pull one out of harmony with Nature, trapping them into a cycle of worry and negativity. However, the moment the man embraced gratitude, his perspective shifted, restoring his alignment with life's natural flow.

As long as we view our challenges through the lens of negativity, we will continue to be entrapped in them. However, when faced with a difficult situation, focus on the blessings hidden beneath the apparent adversity. Start recognizing Nature's gifts bestowed upon us and approach them with love and gratitude.

Express gratitude for every comfort and the discomforts we experience! While comforts bring us ease, discomforts challenge us to develop virtues and remind us of Nature's gifts. Let us thank Nature, which freely and generously provides us with the essentials such as air, water, sunlight, nourishing fruits, and countless other gifts. Let us thank God for each precious breath that sustains us. Let us be grateful not only to those who bring love and joy but also to those who help us learn precious life lessons.

By expressing gratitude for every aspect of life, we enter a state of grace and profound gratefulness, aligning ourselves with God. This alignment draws positivity and abundance toward us, enabling us to bloom fully and open our hearts to life's wonders. In this state of inner blossoming, our lives become no less radiant than those of enlightened beings like the Buddha, the Mahavira, or Saint Meera.

Points for Contemplation:

- Do you feel an alignment with Nature? If so, how do you express gratitude for Nature?
- Think about any incident where you have made a wrong decision. What was the level of awareness at that time? And also, think about the level of awareness when you made a right decision.
- Write a thank-you note for things that didn't seem good at first but turned out to be good later.

13

The Invisible Law Within Gratitude

*"God has two dwellings; one in heaven,
and the other in a meek and thankful heart."*
- Izaak Walton

There was a postman who traveled door-to-door, delivering mail in a small village. On the day of Diwali (Indian festival), he went around not only to deliver mail but also to collect his Diwali gifts from the villagers. At one house, he knocked and waited patiently, but no one answered.

Growing frustrated, he muttered under his breath, "I have so much work… wandering from door to door… if every house takes this long, how will I deliver all the mail?" As he grumbled, a soft voice called out from inside, "Coming… please wait for a moment."

When the door finally opened, the postman saw a disabled girl approaching him with the support of crutches. Seeing her, his complaints instantly ceased. A wave of profound gratitude washed over him as he thought, "It took her five minutes just to reach the door, yet here I am, blessed with strong legs that can carry me a half kilometer in that time. Thank you, God, from the bottom of my heart."

The postman chose not to ask the girl for a Diwali gift or tip. Instead, the girl apologized for her delay, promptly paid for the parcel, received her mail, and thanked him warmly.

A week later, the postman returned to her house to deliver mail. As he approached, the girl noticed he was still wearing the old, worn-out slippers from last time. Silently, she felt a deep gratitude for his unwavering dedication and service. Once he left, she discreetly measured the footprints he left on the ground and sent her friend to the market with those measurements to buy him a new pair of slippers.

After a month, when the postman returned with another parcel, she handed him a small package and smiled. "This is for you. Open it when you get home," she said. When he opened it, he found a brand-new pair of slippers. Tears welled up in his eyes as he realized, "My slippers are torn and worn out, yet even my children did not notice. But this young girl, who barely knows me, understood my hardship and demonstrated such kindness and consideration." As he slipped them on, he realized they fit perfectly. Deeply touched, the postman silently thanked the girl.

The next day, he went to the bank in the district office to request a loan. The bank manager said, "You have already taken out a loan for your son's education. Another loan would significantly impact your finances, potentially consuming all your salary for repayment." The postman replied, "This loan is for someone who cannot walk yet noticed the pain in my legs. I walked in the scorching sun and muddy rain, but she sensed my struggle when we met. I need this loan to buy prosthetic legs for that girl, who is now like a daughter to me."

The postman's words moved the manager deeply. "Why delay such a noble deed when it's within my discretion to approve it?" he said. "You will have the loan right away. Thank you for giving me the opportunity to support this noble cause."

The postman had heard that Jaipur, Rajasthan, was renowned for producing prosthetic limbs. He arranged for a pair perfectly suited to the girl's age and size. A few days later, the new limbs arrived, and she took her first steps with her new legs. Both the postman and girl shed tears of joy and gratitude. In that unforgettable moment, a

The Miracle of Gratitude - 75

beautiful gratitude for gratitude itself shined in its purest and most heartfelt form.

In this way, **when gratitude flows from a pure heart, it radiates into the Universe and returns to us manifold, enriching our lives according to the Laws of Nature.**

The postman's gratitude for his legs brought him a new pair of slippers—an act of pure love that met his need even without asking for it. Similarly, the girl received prosthetic legs, fulfilling her heartfelt wish. Both held pure intentions. It was not that the postman expressed gratitude, expecting slippers. He was expressing his appreciation to God for what he had. Indeed, gratitude enables us to witness Nature's miracles, making us aware of its blessings.

When gratitude arises within, it creates an opportunity for divine qualities to flourish and multiply within us. If you wish for an overflowing abundance, enough to share with others, stay grateful for what you have today. In this state, you invite a multiplication of blessings.

Conversely, if one constantly complains, "Nothing ever goes right for me… people always let me down…this world is a mess…" then Nature mirrors this sentiment by responding, "So be it!" In simple terms, **whatever you focus on intensely is precisely what Nature serves you.**

> There was once a businessman who suffered from persistent pain in the knees. A wise Pandit asked him, "How long have you had this pain?"
>
> The businessman replied, "Look at my plight, Panditji… First, I suffered from backache. Just as that began to improve, my knees started hurting. I even told my doctor that as soon as he fixes one problem, another ailment emerges to take its place."

In this example, the businessman never really saw himself as healthy. His attention was perpetually locked onto his pain with a constant focus on the negative, so Nature echoed back precisely what he was fixated on. However, if one lives in gratitude, recognizing Nature's blessings, Nature multiplies those gifts abundantly in one's life.

Throughout our day, countless little things bring us joy and smiles. Yet, how often do we take these small blessings for granted? We let them pass without a second thought, failing to appreciate them. However, when we take a moment to thank whatever brightened our day, be it a thing, a person, an animal, or nature, we unleash unseen positive forces around us.

You have likely noticed that when we give importance to someone, they are more likely to act with love and consideration toward us. Gratitude works in the same way. It is like a powerful mantra; when we focus on it, life's blessings begin to unfold themselves in beautiful, unexpected ways.

Health, love, wealth, peace, talents, art, wisdom—whatever you desire in life, begin by expressing gratitude as if these blessings have already arrived in your life. By embracing this mindset, you will soon see these very things manifest in your reality.

If you wish to be surrounded by uplifting and supportive people, start with affirmations like, "Everyone in my life is positive, wise, and peace-loving. They live in love and joy. They walk the path of honesty and truth. They always support me, and because of them, I remain in a state of higher consciousness. Thank you, God, for filling my life with such wonderful people."

Start expressing gratitude with the belief and sense of completeness that good and genuine people have already entered your life. Visualize and feel this reality unfolding before your eyes.

From today, make it a practice to repeat these affirmations in prayer each day:

- Thank You, God, for blessing me with the quality of persistence.
- Thank You for granting me perfect health.
- Thank You for surrounding me with positive, uplifting people.
- Thank You for providing everything I need according to the divine plan.
- Thank You for bringing the best things in the world into my life.
- I am overflowing with abundance in every aspect. Now, I am becoming a means to awaken divine qualities in the lives of others; for that, Thank You… Thank You… Thank You!

A Testimonial of Gratitude

It is the human mind's nature to focus on what we lack, driving us to chase after it with relentless energy. If we fail to attain it, we get disappointed. If we succeed, a new desire arises, and the cycle continues. I, too, was trapped in this relentless pursuit.

However, when I discovered the truth, I realized that by embracing the feeling of gratitude, we remain effortlessly joyful. Nature is abundant with blessings such as air, sunlight, water, soil, plants, trees, and breath. Everything moves in perfect harmony on its own. Each part of our body functions seamlessly. These countless blessings from Nature eloquently demonstrate how deeply God's grace flows in our lives.

Every morning, I rise with a deep sense of gratitude, thinking, "I am alive; thank you for the opportunity to witness another beautiful morning." This heartfelt thankfulness sets the tone for my entire day. A simple habit of offering thanks for the contributions others have made to my life has filled it with unprecedented peace and joy. Through the regular practice of gratitude, I have experienced its transformative power.

It truly amazes me how, by embracing a mindset of gratitude, we become calm and open to the infinite blessings the Universe brings our way! Living in gratitude aligns us with the natural rhythm of life. We begin to feel the tiniest ripples of the Universe, resonate in harmony with them, and watch our happiness multiply many times over.

Consistent practice has taught me that gratitude transcends mere thankfulness. When we immerse ourselves in the feeling of gratitude, everything—people, inanimate objects, nature, and events—feels like an integral part of that divine essence we call God.

Today, my heart overflows with gratitude for the privilege to share my thoughts with you.

- A seeker of Truth

Points for Contemplation:

- Do you feel grateful for all the body parts? Express gratitude for them.
- Do you pray daily? Does your prayer include gratitude for all the qualities you want to manifest in your life?
- How can you use affirmations to bring positive changes in your life?

14

The Importance of Purity in Gratitude

"Gratitude is not only the greatest of virtues, but the parent of all the others.
- Marcus Cicero

Our mind often questions, "What will I gain by doing this? What's in it for me?" It insists, "Only when I receive will I give in return." This transactional attitude of the mind perpetually evaluates every action on the scale of profit and loss.

We are constantly told, "Cultivate an attitude of gratitude. Practice thankfulness. If you want a beautiful home, thank God. If you long for a car, express gratitude to the Divine." Desiring things and giving thanks is neither wrong nor harmful in itself. However, gratitude born from desire lacks its true essence. Pure gratitude is about giving thanks without any string attached. Genuine gratitude, in its highest form, is the kind that holds no expectation or selfish interest. It elevates our consciousness and fosters a deep appreciation for providence within us.

> A businessman began expressing gratitude with a pure heart for all the blessings he had received. Gradually, his business started flourishing. He started living in peace and harmony with his family. Eventually, he became the wealthiest man in town. This inflated his ego, and he began treating those less fortunate than him with cold indifference. His gratitude lost its essence as he failed to grasp the purity of true thankfulness.

Similarly, King Uttanapada, the father of the prodigious Prince Dhruva, initially worshiped the Divine with a sincere heart and was blessed with the wise and noble Princess Suneeti as his queen (Suneeti, in Hindi, means virtuous). However, as his kingdom expanded, so did his ego. In time, people with selfish motives, like Suruchi, entered his life (Suruchi implies being overpowered by sensory temptations).

In both these cases, the moment our intentions shift, the consequences become clear. Therefore, gratitude should be offered without conditions or selfish interest. When practiced sincerely, gratitude transforms our feelings and mindset, attuning us to the highest gifts of life.

When gratitude hinges on fulfilling personal desires, it fails to become an integral part of our being. Once those desires are met, our sense of gratitude can vanish. But if we express gratitude from a pure heart and remain thankful regardless of fulfillment, we begin to witness the true miracle of gratitude. In essence, genuine gratitude requires a pure mind, devoid of expectations.

When our hearts overflow with gratitude, we become free from ego and complaint, and we begin to recognize the countless blessings in our lives. This shift purifies the mind and elevates our perspective, filling our hearts with a sincere love for the Divine. This is the true magic of gratitude! The fundamental purpose of human life is to cultivate a loving, pure, and unshakable mind in this very life, and gratitude becomes a powerful ally on this journey. The other blessings we receive through gratitude are simply bonuses.

When we sincerely thank God without expectations, love, joy, and positivity naturally flow into our lives. While love, peace, health, prosperity, and respect come our way, our gratitude focuses solely on reveling in the experience of inner bliss.

When we reflect on the lives of great saints like Saint Tulsidas, Saint Surdas, Meera, and Ramakrishna Paramhansa, we see a striking similarity in their inner states. They perpetually reveled in divine rapture and were grateful to God for the blessing of devotion. Their divine devotion has kept their stories alive, inspiring generations.

From this moment on, express sincere gratitude to God for every small blessing bestowed upon you. For example, you might say, "Dear God, I am grateful to have been born into this wondrous creation with a human body and to witness Nature's incredible miracles." Or "Thank you for the sorrow, for it taught me the value of joy."

Make it a habit to begin each day by expressing gratitude for the blessings showered upon you.

A Testimonial of Gratitude

In the past, whenever I made a mistake, I would feel guilty. I would feel disappointed if I missed waking up early or skipped yoga or meditation. Conversely, whenever I accomplished something positive, like treating others kindly, sending good wishes, completing my morning walk, or practicing yoga, a sense of pride would arise within me, and my mind would say, "I did all this!" Thus, subtle sense of doership and self-arrogation crept in.

However, when I came to understand true gratitude, I realized that waking up early, going for a walk, meditating, or praying is only possible by grace. Nature, or the Divine, grants us the thoughts that inspire us to act. Life is being guided, and the divine essence enables our bodies to perform these actions. For this profound understanding, endless gratitude is owed to Nature, to the Divine.

A deeper understanding has begun to blossom, a realization that "Actions are simply unfolding through me by grace." This insight has infused a constant sense of gratitude throughout my days. When I or someone else makes a mistake, guilt or blame no longer cast their shadows, only gratitude prevails.

In the past, I felt guilty if I overindulged in a delicious meal or spent too much time watching TV. Now, I use these moments as opportunities to cultivate mindfulness. A prayer naturally arises within me: "O Divine Nature, thank you for guiding me toward the highest choices in every moment."

In this way, my words and emotions have begun to change, bringing greater clarity into my life. Through this simple practice, I can see

how beautifully Nature orchestrates life. Not only am I grateful for the better actions happening through this body but also thankful for the continued guidance toward even greater actions and the gradual elevation of my consciousness.

In essence, the ego that once relentlessly stamped every action with a sense of ownership is gradually dissolving. For this profound awakening, I offer my heartfelt gratitude to the power guiding us ever higher, drawing us toward the ultimate.

- A seeker of Truth

Points for Contemplation:

- Do you express gratitude with the expectation of something in return?
- Express sincere gratitude to God for every small blessing bestowed upon you.
- What is pure gratitude? Express pure gratitude for at least one minute.

15

The Role of Faith in Gratitude

"I would maintain that thanks are the highest form of thought, and that gratitude is happiness doubled by wonder."
- Gilbert K. Chesterton

To truly experience and appreciate the transformative cycle of Nature, we must first intentionally cultivate gratitude. Initially, we might not be accustomed to it; we might express gratitude mechanically. However, with persistence, genuine gratitude emerges, fostering self-belief. With the blossoming of self-belief arises inspired action. With each action, our faith strengthens, guiding us deeper into the practice of gratitude.

The journey of gratitude unfolds through five essential stages: feeling, self-belief, action, bright faith (the state of unshakable conviction, beyond belief and doubt), and the transformative impact of gratitude.

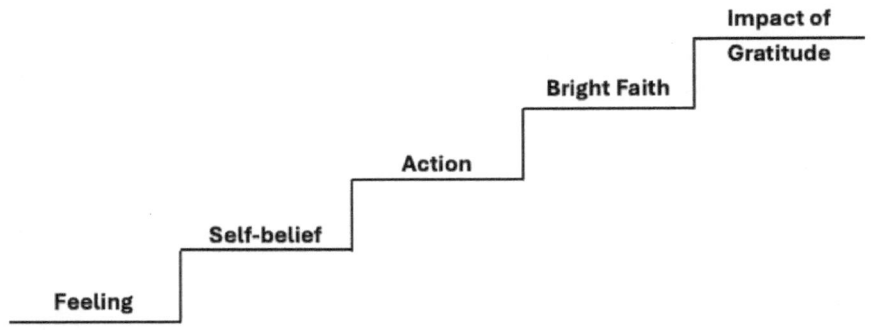

A student struggling with family issues aspired to succeed in his exams but lacked the funds for quality coaching. Amid his struggles, he was introduced to the practice of gratitude. Initially, he doubted its potency, but following the guidance, he began expressing thanks, even if it felt mechanical and lacked genuine feeling. Over time, his gratitude deepened, becoming heartfelt and carrying genuine **feelings**. As a result, helpful study notes unexpectedly came his way, reinforcing his belief in the practice of gratitude.

As his gratitude practice deepened, he received help from senior students. Later, he met a retired teacher who offered him free coaching. His gratitude transformed into a sincere, heartfelt prayer as he thanked God wholeheartedly for his impending success, empowered by the invisible Law of Nature: **As is your feeling, so shall be its outcome.**

Success was within reach for this student. He began taking the necessary steps, turning intention into action. He created a study schedule, allocated time to each subject, and committed to regular study sessions.

As a result, he started scoring well in his preliminary class tests. Witnessing these positive outcomes, his **belief** in the power of gratitude strengthened, and his commitment to the practice deepened, initiating a positive cycle. His consistent **actions** transformed into **bright faith**—a state of unshakable conviction in divine providence, transcending beliefs and doubts. Bright faith elevated his gratitude to a profound height. What began as a simple mechanical act inspired by someone's suggestion ultimately became a powerful tool, contributing to his success. He achieved top exam scores. In other words, the transformative **impact of gratitude** eventually manifested.

With genuine faith, everything becomes possible. Nature is eager to provide everything we desire according to our divine plan; it only needs our gratitude to be rooted in faith. Action serves as a bridge to bring our desire to fruition. When we have **faith** in our dreams, **trust** in our goals, and take the necessary steps toward them, we enter the realm of **action** and experience the magic through the transformative practice of **gratitude**.

There is, however, another side to this story. Imagine a student who desires success and is introduced to the practice of gratitude but approaches it half-heartedly. He follows instructions and writes lines of thanks each morning and evening, yet he recites them mechanically, without faith. Lacking genuine belief in those words, he takes no meaningful action, no concrete steps to reach his goals. Without sincere intention, he begins to doubt himself, thinking, "Can I really succeed?" This breeds self-doubt instead of self-belief, preventing him from making any plans or forming a strategy. His gratitude remains hollow, a mere formality. Without faith and action, Nature does not receive the clear signals needed to respond and support him.

Thus, the student who practiced gratitude with full faith and purposeful actions unlocked a chain of possibilities. In contrast, the one who treated it as an empty formality missed the true power of gratitude. This comparison reveals that gratitude, when embraced with genuine feeling and coupled with purposeful action, becomes a profound force in shaping one's life.

Let us explore this Law of Nature through another example. Many of us express gratitude for our health, but our faith begins to waver at the first sign of a cold or a sniffle, and our gratitude diminishes. In those moments, we forget that the rest of our body still functions perfectly despite the cold.

Now, imagine that along with expressing gratitude for our health, we cultivate unwavering faith that: "I am healthy, and I make wise choices for my body through exercise and nutrition." We support our faith with purposeful actions like regulating our diet, maintaining our exercises, and taking necessary medication. This kind of trust fosters steady confidence within us. Consequently, the gratitude we express becomes genuine rather than superficial. We realize that Nature is always ready to support us, consistently gifting us with the treasure of good health.

This is the Law of Nature. Those who understand and live by it rise to new heights and fulfill life's true purpose. By weaving faith and action into our practice of gratitude, we elevate ourselves in all five facets of life—physical, mental, social, financial, and spiritual.

When we approach life with a heart filled with gratitude for what we seek and move forward with full faith, taking each step intentionally, we discover that our wishes are fulfilled in wondrous ways.

Points for Contemplation:

- Refer to the five stages of the journey of gratitude. On which level are you?
- What actions can you take to go to the next stage?

PART 3

When and Whom to Thank

16

Be Grateful for Your Body

"Gratitude is the art of living life to the fullest."
- Anonymous

Imagine an employee who works tirelessly, without complaining, fulfilling every responsibility with integrity. You never have to explain things to them repeatedly. Yet, you rarely pay full attention to them, never appreciate them, or give them a pat on the back. Instead, sometimes you silently criticize them, thinking, "He is so dark... He is too short... He is so fat." Reflect on this.

This loyal "employee" is none other than our own body. We find it so easy to thank others, yet how often, since we became aware of our existence, have we genuinely thanked our own body? Our body is our closest and only constant friend, unwavering in its support through every action we take and every decision we make. Yet, are we truly grateful for it?

In reality, gratitude is not a habit that comes to us naturally. Instead, it is an inner feeling, a sense of joy, love, and respect that finds expression through the words "Thank you." Let us explore this understanding from several angles.

When we want to play cricket, football, tennis, or any sport, our body assists us. When we decide to study for two hours or meditate for an hour, our body helps us with that, too. From morning till night, we make it perform countless tasks. Beyond these, our body performs some critical functions involuntarily and tirelessly, without our instruction, like the heart beating, lungs breathing, kidneys filtering impurities, and so on.

Even the most advanced machines in the world cannot match the miracles our body performs every single day. But have we ever truly thanked our body? Do we even pause once a day to acknowledge our organs? The truth is, where our attention goes, our energy follows. The attention we give is, in itself, an expression of gratitude. By being mindful, we infuse each part of our body with energy, showing that we recognize, appreciate, and are deeply grateful for all that it does for us.

Now, this raises a question: Can we express gratitude to our body simply by saying "Thank you," or are there other meaningful ways? Yes, there are indeed many ways. We can allow our organs to feel cherished and cared for through love and appreciation. Let us explore some ways to do this.

1. When we engage in *Pranayama* or physical exercises like *Yoga* with focused awareness on each body part, we bring our attention to these areas, allowing them to feel invigorated. Physical activity keeps the body healthy, and activities like climbing stairs, taking walks, swimming, going to the gym, or practicing Pranayama, every effort we make to keep our body healthy is an act of gratitude.

2. When we are working continuously and our body begins to feel fatigued, simply taking a break to rest and rejuvenate is another way of thanking it.

3. Regularly caring for each part of our body, soothing it with love, keeping it clean, nourishing it with wholesome, pure food, massaging it, telling it "I love you," and responding to its needs are all ways to show appreciation. Listening to our body's signals, whether they are a sensation of pain or discomfort, and responding to and treating them rather than ignoring them are all forms of gratitude toward the body.

Let us understand this with an example to illustrate how we often overlook what the body is trying to communicate.

Imagine you have a sweet tooth and enjoy a *laddoo* (Indian sweet) with delight. Your body helps digest it, allowing you to feel satisfied. However, when you continue indulging, eating one laddoo after another, eventually, your body will try to signal, "That's enough." Yet, lost in the pleasure, you ignore this signal. At that moment, you do not realize how much strain it places on your body to digest excess food. In this way, unintentionally, we bring pain and discomfort to our body, which is the opposite of gratitude. Eating mindfully, according to need and nourishment, is a proper way to honor and thank our body.

Allowing ourselves to dwell in prolonged worry and stress inevitably takes a toll on our body, leaving us feeling unwell and depleted. This highlights why it is essential to stay mindful of our actions, understand which ones nourish, uplift, and restore the body, and which ones burden or strain it. Put simply, we must recognize which actions serve as gratitude for the body and which create hardship.

When we use our senses with purpose and mindfulness, we express gratitude to the body. Speaking kind, uplifting words is an act of gratitude, whereas indulging in gossip or criticism reflects thanklessness. Similarly, maintaining a disciplined daily routine is a powerful way to thank the body.

At this point, you might wonder, "Why show gratitude for a body that's unwell?" The presence of illness means it is time to give the body even more attention and care, it is a time to deepen our gratitude. During such times, express as much thanks and love to your body as possible. Silently say, "Thank you, my healthy and beautiful companion, for all you are and everything you keep doing for me."

Nature multiplies whatever we are genuinely grateful for in our lives. So, when you express gratitude for your health, you welcome more health and vitality. You will fall ill less often, and even if you do fall sick, you will recover quickly.

We have been bestowed with this precious human body. Those who comprehend its significance are indeed worthy of praise. Let today be the turning point for those who have not yet grasped its depth. Begin now to offer thanks to your body. To assist in this, we can also practice meditation, which will be discussed in the next chapter.

A Testimonial of Gratitude

During the COVID-19 pandemic, I was infected by the virus and was overwhelmed with fear and anxiety. In that state of distress, I began silently repeating affirmations based on my Guru's teachings: "I am God's treasure; no negative force can touch me, and nothing will ever harm me." Then, as if guided by the Divine, a message from my Guru about gratitude appeared on YouTube. I listened to it intently, and it started completely transforming my perspective. The results began to show. Although I had practiced gratitude since childhood, I couldn't recall it amidst the stress and illness. This message reminded me of the profound power of gratitude.

From that moment on, I made expressing gratitude a regular part of my daily routine. I thanked my body, bed, doctors, nurses, helpers, and family members for supporting me. Within four to five days, I began to feel better. My body started to heal gradually, and I noticed that every time I expressed heartfelt gratitude, a deep sense of peace, satisfaction, and faith blossomed within me.

Slowly but surely, everything began to flow smoothly and effortlessly. For all this, I was filled with immense gratitude for God. In this way, gratitude has brought miracles into my life.

- A seeker of Truth

Points for Contemplation:

- How do you show your gratitude to your body?
- Are you able to thank your body even during illness?

17

Gratitude Meditation for the Body

*"Thankfulness is the key to a healthy and happy life,
which helps us experience joy every single day."*
- **Anonymous**

The human body is a sacred temple of the supreme power, housing the eternal flame of consciousness that burns brightly within. Therefore, we must keep this sacred vessel healthy and active.

Let us embark on a meditation practice to express gratitude for the body.

This practice will guide in developing love and appreciation for your body. When the body is infused with the energy of love and gratitude, it naturally strengthens, creating a shield against illnesses. Even in sickness, this meditation can catalyze healing and restoration.

If you ever feel disheartened by comparing your body to someone else's, wondering, "Why isn't my body as healthy or beautiful as theirs?" it is time to change this misguided perception. Right here and now, affirm, "My body is my dearest friend. I accept it completely, exactly as it is. It stands by me unconditionally in every situation, and for this, I feel deep love and gratitude."

A Testimonial of Gratitude

During a medical examination, I was diagnosed with a severe disease called rheumatoid arthritis. My doctor warned me that I might eventually need a wheelchair. But I firmly declared to myself and my doctor, "Not only will I walk independently, but I will also run marathons, cycle, and even climb Mt. Everest!"

I began taking Ayurvedic treatment for my condition and, by divine grace, had the opportunity to meet His Holiness the Dalai Lama. He directed me to a Tibetan physician. The physician looked serious upon assessing my condition. Undeterred, I encouraged him to share his honest feedback about my illness. Simultaneously, I silently kept affirming to myself, "I will heal myself by staying joyful and maintaining unwavering faith."

From that moment, I adopted a mindset of gratitude and embraced joy in every moment. Gradually, I began to feel my body's cells regenerating and becoming healthier. Today, I am living my everyday life with ease and comfort.

- A seeker of Truth

Gratitude meditation for the body

Let us begin the Gratitude Meditation for the body. The purpose of this meditation is to express sincere gratitude toward your body. First, read and fully understand the steps of the meditation, and then practice it. If you wish, record these instructions in your own voice and play them as you meditate.

1. Find a neat, clean, and tranquil place to sit peacefully. Settle into a comfortable position, such as *Sukhasana* or any meditative pose that feels right for you. Breathe in deeply, exhale slowly, and gently close your eyes.

2. Allow your entire body to relax deeply. Now, recall the profound feeling you experienced when you held a little child for the first time or the warmth and unconditional love you felt while cuddling in your parents' embrace.

3. Immerse yourself in that beautiful feeling of love and let it create a sense of harmony between your body and mind. Silently affirm to yourself, "My body is perfectly healthy, and I love myself deeply. Thank you... Thank you... Thank you..."

4. Gently bring your attention to your five senses, remembering that where your focus goes, your energy flows. These senses are the gateways of your expression and connection with the world. As you focus on each sense one by one, reflect on its magnificence:

   - Our eyes allow us to witness the beauty of this world.
   - The ears help us receive verbal instructions, enjoy music, and immerse ourselves in the teachings of wisdom.
   - The nose is the channel for breathing, filtering the air as it enters and leaves. It enables the flow of life force within us and helps us enjoy the various fragrances of nature.
   - The tongue allows us to savor delicious and nourishing food and to express love and kindness through speech.
   - Our skin gives us the joy of feeling. Through our touch, we convey feelings of love, compassion, sympathy, appreciation, and greetings to others. The physical touch also helps us perceive the softness of flowers, the hardness of stone, the warmth of sunlight, and the cool breeze. It also senses changes in the surroundings, such as heat, cold, or dryness.

   How dull and incomplete life would be if even one of these senses were to stop functioning, even for a day? Allow gratitude to rise in your heart for each sense and let your love flow toward them. Silently affirm, "Dear senses, I thank you for allowing me to experience the beauty and diversity of life so fully. I am deeply grateful for each of you."

5. Now, shift your focus to your head. Visualize your hair, a beautiful shield that protects and adorns you. Your hair guards you from environmental changes, like the sun's rays, the cold wind, or the rain. Imagine caressing it gently, saying inwardly, "Thank you... Thank you... Thank you..."

6. Shift your attention to your precious brain. Fill your heart with love for it, being as tender and caring for it as if you were speaking to someone

you hold dear. Silently tell your brain: "Dearest brain, I thank you from the bottom of my heart. You work tirelessly for me, offering clarity of thought and helping me make wise decisions every single day. I love you deeply. Thank you… Thank you… Thank you…" Stay immersed in this feeling of love and gratitude for a few moments.

7. Gently bring your attention to your neck and throat. Reflect on how they support your voice, enabling you to express yourself. Within your throat lies the remarkable thyroid gland, which plays a vital role by sending hormones to the brain, ensuring your body functions smoothly. With deep gratitude and love, silently say, "Dear neck and throat, I love you so much. Thank you… Thank you… Thank you…" Stay immersed in this energy of love for some time, then move on to your hands.

8. Now, turn your awareness to your shoulders, upper arms, elbows, wrists, and fingers. These body parts allow you to create, hold, and accomplish countless daily tasks. For that, fill your heart with love and appreciation as you acknowledge them and silently say, "Thank you… Thank you… Thank you…"

9. Shift your attention to your chest. Within it lies your lungs, vital for breathing, and your heart, which pumps blood throughout your body. This is also the center from which you give and receive the energy of love. Feel the warmth of gratitude radiating from within. Place your hands gently on your chest and silently say, "Thank you… Thank you… Thank you…"

10. Next, focus on your abdomen. Your entire digestive system resides here, including your stomach, liver, small and large intestines, kidneys, and pancreas. These organs work tirelessly to convert food into nourishment and cleanse your body of impurities. As Ayurveda teaches, "A healthy gut is the foundation of overall health." Let gratitude flow through you as you silently say, "Thank you for always supporting and nourishing me. Thank you… Thank you… Thank you…"

11. Next, bring awareness to your hips, waist, thighs, and reproductive organs. These parts play essential roles in movement and stability and ensure the human race's continuation. Often overlooked, they quietly support you every moment. Shower them with love and appreciation, and silently say, "Thank you… Thank you… Thank you…"

12. Focus on your knees, calves, and feet, the steadfast pillars of your movement and exploration. They enable you to walk, run, travel, exercise, and discover the world. Silently bearing the weight of your entire body, they support you with every step of your journey. Acknowledge this and let your heart fill with profound gratitude, silently affirming, "Thank you for your strength, resilience, and unwavering support. Thank you… Thank you… Thank you…" Envelop your knees, calves, and feet with love and appreciation.

13. Another vital part of the body that deserves special care and affection is the spine, the pillar of the body that provides structure and support. Gently shift your attention to it and shower it with abundant love and gratitude. Silently say to your spine, "May you remain strong and healthy, supporting my entire body gracefully. I love you deeply. Thank you… Thank you… Thank you…"

14. Now, maintain the energy of love and gratitude you have cultivated. Visualize your entire body once more in your mind, and gently say, "My beloved body, I honor and cherish you. I deeply love this sacred temple that carries me through life. I ask for your forgiveness if I have ever

caused you harm, knowingly or unknowingly. May you remain healthy, vibrant, and full of life. Thank you... Thank you... Thank you..."

15. Stay in this state of gratitude and love for a while, allowing the energy to settle within you. Then, slowly take a deep, steady breath and gently open your eyes as you exhale. Look at your body with wonder, acknowledging its magnificence and the miracle of its existence.

From this moment on, cultivate the practice of expressing gratitude to every part of your body, both inside and out. Care for it with devotion, cherish it with love and honor it with kindness every day.

Through the power of this practice, you can overcome any illness or discomfort. If a specific area of your body is in pain or distress, dedicate extra time to focus on it to enable healing. Shower it with love, sincerely apologize for any harm caused, and infuse it with the transformative energy of gratitude.

Points for Contemplation:

- Do you compare your body with others?
- What did you learn from this meditation? Please continue this gratitude and love for your body throughout the day.

18

Gratitude for the Tools That Serve Us

"Gratitude is the beginning, Gratitude is the conclusion, Gratitude is the mother of complete success."
- **Anonymous**

Mahesh was rushing to the office when a sudden downpour caught him off guard. To make matters worse, his car stalled in the middle of the road. His frustration mounted as he tried to start it repeatedly, but it refused to budge. In a fit of anger, Mahesh stepped out, kicked the car, and shouted, "Why did you have to break down now?" Although Mahesh might have been in a rush, was his reaction appropriate?

Now consider Ramesh. He owned an old car that he cleaned diligently with care every morning. As he caressed it, he would say, "You have been my constant companion. Through the chill of winter, the heat of summer, storms, and rain, you have taken me everywhere on time." Ramesh's gratitude forged a connection with his car, making it his ally.

Today, machines and gadgets, both large and small, have become an essential part of our lives, making everything remarkably convenient. Reflecting on their contribution naturally stirs a sense of thankfulness. Consider the mobile phone, which allows us to connect with anyone, anywhere, with just a few taps. Isn't that amazing? Why not acknowledge its service with a simple, heartfelt thought like, "Thank you, my friend, for keeping me connected."

Every inanimate object that tirelessly serves us—our homes, cars, phones, appliances, or tools—deserves our respect and gratitude. Care for them lovingly, maintain them thoughtfully, and honor their role in your life. When you do so, even these seemingly lifeless objects begin to resonate with your energy, aligning themselves with you in harmony. Let us take a moment to express gratitude for the many tools and objects that make our lives more comfortable and efficient.

Even modern science agrees that everything in existence, including inanimate objects like stones, carries energy vibrations. When we use our belongings with gratitude, they respond to our energy, functioning more smoothly and harmoniously.

How many objects do we rely on from the moment we wake up until we go to bed? Even while we sleep, appliances like fans, air conditioners, and air coolers work tirelessly to ensure we rest peacefully through the night. Have you ever taken a moment in the morning to thank them? If not, start today. Say something as simple as, "Thank you for keeping my room cool and allowing me to rest comfortably. Your service rejuvenates my body and mind."

Also, express gratitude to your phone, a constant companion that works round-the-clock to simplify your life. It does so much for you: connecting you with others, handling your finances, storing important documents, and even enabling you to join meetings or complete office tasks remotely. From entertainment to keeping you informed about global events, your phone serves you in countless ways.

When gratitude takes root in our hearts, it naturally transforms how we relate to our belongings. We become mindful of their care, recognizing their importance in our lives, no matter how large or small they are. Whether it is a pair of shoes, slippers, your phone, your laptop, or your car, every object holds its unique significance in your life.

Caring for these possessions with love and respect is a profound way of expressing gratitude. Even when an object has served its purpose and is replaced or discarded, let us part with it in gratitude, acknowledging the role it played in our journey. Cleaning, storing, and using them mindfully is a form of thanksgiving.

A Testimonial of Gratitude

The difference between the life I once lived without gratitude and the life I lead now, embracing gratitude, is as vast as the distance between the earth and the sky.

I rode a motor scooter a while ago but always longed to drive a car. I joined driving schools several times, yet an underlying fear always held me back. I often vented my frustration on my scooter and felt increasingly irritated whenever I saw my car in the parking space that I could not drive.

When I learned the importance of gratitude from my guru, I gained profound insights and understood that even inanimate objects are a form of consciousness. They respond to our praise, anger, or neglect. Gradually, I began expressing my gratitude toward my scooter and car with these words:

"O God, thank you for this scooter that carries me where I need to go, allowing me to navigate through traffic with such ease and reliability. This scooter has served me tirelessly for years, and I am deeply grateful for its service. I humbly seek forgiveness from the bottom of my heart for moments when I have directed anger toward my scooter, knowingly or unknowingly. I am profoundly grateful to my guru for imparting the wisdom I needed at the right moment."

With this newfound awareness, I began to pray with sincerity: "O God, please grant me the confidence to drive this car without fear. I thank you and this car for this blessing.

This car has silently endured my anger and frustration. I sincerely apologize for that. I express my heartfelt gratitude with faith that it will continue to serve me well."

When I began praying this way, what followed was nothing short of a miracle. Within just a month, I found myself effortlessly learning to drive. The fear that had once held me captive disappeared, replaced by confidence and ease. Today, I can travel independently and confidently. Now, I make it a point to express daily gratitude to my vehicles and all the objects that support me. I have understood how significant their profound presence is in my life. This extraordinary transformation through the practice of gratitude has indeed been a revelation.

- A seeker of Truth

Where to begin

Let us embark on this journey of gratitude by reflecting on something that plays a significant role in our daily lives: the pen we use.

A pen, simple and unassuming, carries immense significance. It has the power to write history, spark revolutions, and promote global peace. Imagine a student in the midst of an important exam whose pen suddenly stops working. In that moment of need, the true value of this everyday tool becomes clear. While it may seem small, easily replaceable, and readily available, a pen holds tremendous importance, particularly when it serves us at crucial times.

 Today, let us use this example to understand how we can cultivate gratitude for the objects that assist us. Before or after using your pen, take a moment to hold it gently and say with heartfelt emotion, "My dear pen, my trusted companion, you write so beautifully. Whenever you are in my hand, you inspire me with fresh ideas and help me express myself clearly. You are an essential part of my life. Thank you for supporting me in my writing endeavors!"

A Testimonial of Gratitude

I am a 21-year-old student, and for years, I have struggled with an unusual problem—every object that comes into my possession seems to either break or stop working. My family is well aware of this and avoids giving me anything new to use.

My aunt visited us for a few days last summer. She is a cheerful, kind-hearted woman who is always eager to help others. Her personality radiates positive energy, and everyone enjoys her presence.

One sunny afternoon, I enthusiastically told my family, "Today, I will make mango shakes for everyone!" Their joy was heartwarming, and their excitement fueled my own. With great enthusiasm, I went to the market and carefully selected ripe mangoes, creamy milk, and a tub of ice cream to create the perfect treat.

Back home, I meticulously prepared everything. However, as soon as I turned on the blender, it whirred for a moment and then stopped. Frustrated, I banged the blender, unplugged it, re-plugged it, and tried again, but to no avail. My frustration boiled over, and I muttered angrily, "Why does this always happen to me?"

At that moment, my aunt entered the kitchen. She gently touched my shoulder and said lovingly, "Let me take a look. You step back for a moment." Her calming touch diffused my anger slightly, and I stepped aside to observe her.

I noticed something remarkable that day. She handled every item with care and affection, even the mango peels! She touched the blender jar and the blender itself as if they were cherished friends. Then, with utmost patience, she examined the blender's base, pressed the reset button, and switched it on. To my amazement, the blender whirred back to life! She smiled as she effortlessly prepared the mango shake while I stood dumbfounded.

The following day, my parents had to leave for a few days due to urgent work. That day profoundly changed how I perceived the world. Once we were alone, I confided in her about my recurring problem. She listened patiently and then introduced me to the concept of gratitude.

She said, "Every object, no matter how small or insignificant it may seem, deserves our respect and gratitude. When we treat things with love, how we touch and handle them changes. This love not only fills us with positivity but also resonates with the objects, even though they are inanimate. In their own mysterious ways, these objects respond to our love and gratitude by working harmoniously with us."

My aunt did not simply explain the concept of gratitude; she encouraged me to experience it firsthand through practical application. She said, "Do not blindly accept what I say. Test it yourself with small experiments and learn its truth through your own experience. Whether it is a simple pen or a laptop, when you touch it, remember that 'This is my helping hand and it plays an essential role in my life.' Whisper a heartfelt 'I love you' to it and observe. You will sense the impact of your transformed feelings on these inanimate objects."

She added, "Your attitude creates a ripple of energy in the environment, causing everything around you to function more smoothly. Even when something breaks or ceases to work, you will still feel gratitude for the service it provided."

Today, I am filled with immense happiness. Everything my aunt taught me has proven to be 100% true. I discovered this through personal experimentation and by actively applying these lessons during the last year. Today, even when my pen runs out of ink, I feel grateful as I discard it. It is beautiful for one living being to express gratitude to another. However, I have learned that offering gratitude to inanimate objects can also change our lives profoundly. It can shift our mindset, transform our thoughts, and even spread love within our hearts. This realization came to me just a few days ago, and it has deeply impacted my perspective.

- A seeker of Truth

Points for Contemplation:

- Did you know that all our belongings are filled with energy, and they respond to our feelings?
- Express gratitude for each item you use daily.

19

Gratitude for Those Who Teach Us How to Live

"We should all be thankful for those people who rekindle the inner spirit."
- Albert Schweitzer

Once, a king was traveling through his kingdom with his cavalcade. Along the way, they passed a lush mango orchard. Suddenly, out of nowhere, a stone struck the king's forehead, leaving him in pain. Alarmed, the soldiers rushed to find the culprit. Moments later, they returned with a trembling seven-year-old boy in tow, accusing him of the act and demanding his punishment.

Curious and slightly astonished, the king asked the boy, "Why did you throw a stone at me?" The boy replied with innocent eyes and a trembling voice, "Please forgive me, Your Majesty. I didn't mean to hurt you. I was aiming at the mango tree, hoping to get a mango, but instead, the stone hit you. I didn't even get a mango; to make matters worse, your soldiers have caught me!"

After listening to the child, the king felt a voice stir within his heart: "If a tree gives fruits even to those who throw stones at it, then why should man, the most precious creation of God, repay harm with harm? Nature wants to provide us good things in every situation." The king learned a vital lesson. In return, he ordered that the child be given a basket of mangoes.

This story is not just a lesson for the king; it holds profound wisdom for all of us. When someone plays a negative role in our lives or does something that disturbs us, instead of reacting with anger or hurt, we should consider that something better is undoubtedly hidden behind this experience. Whatever is happening now is perfect. When we learn to view events with this perspective, we begin to appreciate the divine play of life. We rise above the labels of positive and negative, and instead of reacting, we respond with gratitude.

Adverse circumstances and undesirable people enter our lives as challenges. If we are troubled by them, we need to step back and view the situation differently. Instead of reacting with anger or complaints, we might silently offer gratitude. Every challenge, no matter how uncomfortable, holds the potential to teach invaluable life lessons.

Consider the life of Lord Rama. Had Manthara and Queen Kaikeyi not played their negative roles, would his exile to the forest have been possible? Would the sages and ascetics, who fervently prayed for years to catch a glimpse of Lord Rama, have been blessed by his presence? Could anyone else in the kingdom have said, "Lord Rama, go to the forest and uplift the sages and seekers there"?

Similarly, by playing his role as the antagonist by abducting Sita, Ravana became an essential part of the divine narrative. Without him, how many devotees would have missed their opportunity to witness the divine drama unfold? The very challenges he created opened pathways for many to experience and appreciate Lord Rama's noble and righteous presence. The same holds true for Lord Krishna's life. For the world to witness the expression of Lord Krishna's divine virtues, Kansa had to assume the role of the villain in the story. Similarly, it was due to the enmity of the Kauravas that the Pandavas had the opportunity to demonstrate their nobility, righteousness, and unwavering faith.

If you observe closely, life resembles a two-hour movie, complete with a hero and a villain. Through their interaction, we understand the interplay of good and evil, bringing the story to life. The hero's qualities shine brightly only when contrasted against the villain's darkness. Yet, behind the scenes, the actors portraying these opposing roles often share camaraderie and laughter, reminding us of a profound truth. Every individual has come to Earth to play a role, and each role, whether positive or negative, is essential. Each one expresses their essence in a unique way, and for this, we owe them all our gratitude.

Take a moment to reflect on your journey. Haven't the challenges posed by those who seemed to oppose you often propelled you toward success? Haven't these experiences shaped your resilience and stregthened your determination?

Saint Kabir has beautifully captured this in his couplet: *"Nindak niyare rakhiye, aangan kuti chhawaye, Bin paani, sabun bina, nirmal kare subhaaye."*

"Keep your critics close to you; even build them a hut in your courtyard, for without water or soap, they help cleanse your character."

In essence, critics and naysayers, who seem to play a negative role, are essential in our lives and should be kept close. They serve as mirrors, reflecting our flaws and providing us with the opportunity to refine ourselves. We can then work on these shortcomings and transform them into virtues.

A Testimonial of Gratitude

After finishing school, I faced financial difficulties that prevented me from pursuing a graduate degree. Instead, I enrolled in a two-year course and began working immediately.

My job was in the city, far from my village home, making daily commutes impossible. To address this, I relocated to live with my uncle and aunt in the city. This arrangement saved me time, money, and energy while ensuring I reached the office punctually.

For a few days, everything went smoothly. However, my aunt soon began to feel burdened by my stay and eventually refused to let me continue living there. This was deeply hurtful for both my mother and me. With no other options left, I decided to rent a place. A few months later, I brought my sister to the city so she could continue her studies. As time passed, I also relocated my mother to the city.

Today, as I reflect on that chapter of my life, my heart overflows with gratitude for my aunt. Had she not played that so-called negative role back then, my family might never have come together to live in a better place in the city. Those early days were indeed challenging, but they shaped me, taught me invaluable decision-making skills, and ultimately led to a better life for my entire family.

- A seeker of Truth

Try doing this

Find a peaceful, airy space where you can sit comfortably. Close your eyes and let your body and mind relax. Take a deep, steady breath, and then exhale gently. Repeat this three times.

In your mind, visualize three individuals who have played negative roles in your life. Reflect deeply on how their actions have ultimately benefited you and contributed to your growth, strength, or unexpected blessings. With a pure heart and sincere emotion, express your heartfelt gratitude to them for the roles they played.

Here are a few lines you can use to express your gratitude:

"Thank you for being in my life.

Thank you for being the catalyst for transformation in my journey.

Because of you, I found the strength to build a successful career.

You taught me the invaluable lessons of

self-reliance, resilience, and patience.

I am profoundly grateful for this.

Thank you for being the unseen force

behind the joy and prosperity in my life.

I am deeply indebted to you.

Thank you. Thank you. Thank you."

Offer this genuine gratitude to those who have played negative roles in your life. Accept their presence with a sense of acknowledgment and understanding. Look at the complete picture of your life, including its nuances and challenges, and let your heart fill with positive emotions toward them.

After expressing gratitude in your field of attention, if you still sense lingering negativity toward them, it is time to take another transformative step. Beyond thanking them, extend a prayer infused with balance and compassion. Mentally invite them into your field of attention, enveloped in a radiant white light, and bless them:

"You are pure, sacred, and virtuous.

You are a divine being and possess all the divine qualities

that are also present within me.

May God always keep you happy and prosperous.

May your wishes be fulfilled in perfect harmony

according to the divine will.

May you always remain healthy.

With God as my witness, I sincerely seek forgiveness from my heart for any hurt I may have caused you, knowingly or unknowingly, through my feelings, thoughts, words, or actions. Please forgive me. Also, for any pain you may have caused me, knowingly or unknowingly, through your feelings, thoughts, words, or actions, I wholeheartedly forgive you with God as my witness. I now release myself from all negative feelings toward you and free my heart from any burden of resentment."

By offering such a prayer, your feelings toward those who have played negative roles in your life will be transformed. This practice will also help you develop a greater awareness and understanding of those playing similar roles in your present. When you repeat these affirmations sincerely, sacred and uplifting feelings will arise within you. You will gain a profound insight, "The time for change has come. Something within me needs transformation, which is why God has sent this person into my life to challenge me to grow."

Points for Contemplation:

- Haven't the challenges posed by those who seemed to oppose you often propelled you toward success? Haven't these experiences shaped your resilience and sharpened your determination?

- List all the people who have seemingly played a negative role in your life. Pray for them and observe how your feelings toward them change.

20

Instilling Gratitude in Children

"The seed of gratitude yields the harvest of happiness, peace, prosperity, love, and devotion."
- Anonymous

When children learn to live with gratitude from an early age, their lives become richly imbued with divine blessings. They are shielded from the negativity of complaints, stress, despair, and worries about the future. Gratitude fortifies their foundation, ensuring they remain resilient even in the face of life's challenges.

While children are taught to say "Thank you" at school and home as a matter of social etiquette, it has become merely a part of polite conversation. Although it is an integral aspect of social behavior and interactions, it is rarely felt deeply from the heart. Genuine gratitude is a deep-seated feeling that touches the heart. Most children quickly say "Thank you" almost automatically, but that mere verbal expression of gratitude does not fully embody the depth of that sentiment. We must focus on instilling this sentiment in children and, more importantly, practice it ourselves.

When a plate of food is placed before us, many of us, including children, say a quick prayer to thank God for it. Children learn this ritual through observation. Yet, for children to truly feel deep gratitude, we must help them understand the incredible process of how crops are grown, reach the markets, are purchased, and are finally transformed into delicious dishes before being served on our plates.

While children thank God for the food served, they should also extend their gratitude to the farmers who have toiled to grow it, the supply chain that transported it to their town, their parents who bought it, and those who cooked it with care to suit their tastes. In this way, children grasp the significance of gratitude—it is not just about saying "Thank you" but also about thinking of all those who contributed to it. This awareness nurtures respect and realization of the collective effort involved. They will eat their food with a deeper feeling of gratitude and are less likely to waste it.

Similarly, it is essential to inspire children to appreciate the significance of nature. Let them plant a tree themselves and entrust them with the

responsibility of nurturing it. Instill in them the understanding that they are not serving the trees; instead, the trees are selflessly serving us. Trees provide us with fruits, flowers, shade, wood, paper, and life-sustaining oxygen. They protect Mother Earth from the effects of global warming and sustain countless forms of life. When children connect with trees and plants with this understanding, they naturally develop a sense of gratitude and respect for nature and are less likely to harm it.

Take a moment to reflect. Are you connected to the things around you in this manner, or are you in the process of forming that connection? Are you living your life with a sense of gratitude? Children are keen observers, and they learn most effectively through example. If you embody gratitude in your thoughts and actions, they will naturally absorb this quality and awaken to the magical feeling of thankfulness. As a result, children will begin to truly appreciate their parents' boundless love and sacrifices. They will come to understand that their very existence, upbringing, and every small and significant care stem from their parents' unmatched, irreplaceable love. When this feeling touches their hearts, even if there are differences, they are less likely to hurt their parents.

Sow the seed of gratitude in the child's heart with loving care, and their outlook toward life will become positive and enriched.

Encourage children to express gratitude toward other family members as well. Help them understand how grandparents, uncles, aunts, and cousins enrich their lives. Share with them the value of togetherness, the unique role each family member plays, how mutual support fosters harmony, and how joyful it is to come together, share a meal, and sing together. When children experience this warmth, they will feel grateful for their family.

If a child demands something beyond the family's means, gently share with them the realities of the world by citing examples of people who struggle to meet their basic needs like food and shelter. Tell them about a child who yearns for a loaf of bread to satisfy their hunger, in contrast to another child who feels dissatisfied with a small toy and asks for a bigger one. Instead of being upset, scolding them, or denying them outright, use this moment to teach the value of gratitude by encouraging them to express thanks for the toy they already have. Emphasize that having a toy is a privilege that many children do not enjoy. Encourage them to appreciate what they already have. If they still wish for another toy, guide them to frame their desire with gratitude and prayer, saying:

"Dear God,

You gave me this wonderful toy I enjoy playing with.

Thank you very much for this.

I am deeply grateful for this toy.

Now, I wish to experience something new,

so please bless me with a slightly bigger toy."

We know that praying with patience and gratitude can bring about miracles, but it will be a new experience for a child. When the child eventually receives the new toy, their joy will multiply, not only because of the gift itself but also because they will have learned the profound lessons of gratitude and patience.

Stories are among the most effective ways to instill gratitude in children. In the past, grandparents often shared bedtime stories filled with values, morals, and life lessons. Unfortunately, this beautiful tradition is fading away with the rise of nuclear families. However, you can still sow the seeds of virtue in children by sharing stories from books or exploring inspiring content on social media platforms like YouTube. These stories can help children realize the value of gratitude.

Here is one such story to share:

> One morning, a visually impaired boy sat by the roadside, holding a signboard that read, "I am blind. Please help me." In front of him lay a few scattered coins given by passersby.

The Miracle of Gratitude - 115

A man passing by saw the boy and paused. He gently placed some coins on the boy's lap. Then, picking up the signboard, he flipped it over, wrote something new on the blank side, and handed it back to the boy before walking away.

Later that evening, the man returned along the same road and noticed that the boy had collected even more money. Upon hearing the man's footsteps, the boy recognized him and asked, "Sir, were you the one who wrote something on my signboard this morning? What did you write?"

The man replied, "I wrote what was already written on your board but in a different way. I wrote, '**Today is a beautiful day, but I cannot see it. Thank you very much for your help. Enjoy your day!**'"

Both messages conveyed the truth, yet their impact was vastly different. While the first message implied, "The boy is blind; he is helpless," the new message gently reminded people of their own blessings, particularly the gift of sight. It inspired them to feel grateful for what they often took for granted.

This simple yet powerful story beautifully illustrates how even a small shift in perspective can awaken deep gratitude. You can share such inspiring and transformative stories with children. You can also recount real-life incidents where something that initially seemed negative or challenging later revealed an invaluable lesson. By doing so, children will learn to appreciate even unfavorable experiences that lead to deep learning and growth. Over time, this practice will help shape their perspective on life, instilling in them the ability to live with gratitude.

Points for Contemplation:

- Just as children ask curious questions and expect answers, make it a daily practice to ask them thought-provoking questions that help them appreciate how beautiful life is and why they should always be thankful.

- After sharing a story of gratitude, ask them what they learned from it. This will encourage them to contemplate.

- Encourage children to develop a writing habit and inspire them to write a thank-you note every night before going to bed, listing five blessings or lessons from the day for which they are thankful.

21

Being Grateful for Undesirable Events

"Animals live an easy, instinctive life, but the auspicious opportunity for self-realization, the ultimate liberation, is possible only through the human being. So, be grateful for this human life and be mindful to keep it pure and sacred."
- Sirshree

In life, does everything always happen as we desire? Or are there times when the unexpected occurs? When faced with undesirable events, can we express gratitude? In most cases, the answer is no. Gratitude is often the last thing on our minds when things don't go as planned. Instead, we frequently become disappointed, resist the situation, and feel frustrated. We get caught up in a whirlwind of complaints, believing nothing is going right. In such moments, positivity seems elusive, and we cannot even feel thankful. We might wonder, "How can I be grateful for something that disrupts my peace and unsettles my mind?"

Let us understand this through a story.

> Once, a band of treasure hunters discovered an ancient map that promised to lead them to untold riches. They devised a plan and embarked on a journey, following the map step by step. After much effort, they finally arrived at the entrance of a mysterious cave, its massive door etched with intricate symbols and cryptic illustrations. Realizing these were riddles to unlock the cave, they worked tirelessly, deciphering the cryptic clues with unwavering determination. At last, their efforts bore fruit, and the door creaked open, revealing the splendor of untold treasures. Elated, they reveled in their success, marveling at the riches now within their grasp.

However, their jubilation was short-lived. As they tried to leave with their newfound riches, they found that the entrance door had mysteriously closed behind them, trapping them inside. Panic set in as they desperately struggled to open the door, but all their efforts were in vain.

Exhausted and discouraged, they slumped against the unyielding door. As two days passed, despair deepened, and everyone almost lost hope of escape. One of them lamented, "We endured so much to find this treasure, yet it seems our efforts were in vain. If we cannot escape this cave, all this wealth will mean nothing, and we will perish here."

One of the older members of the group sought solace in God. He chose to seek forgiveness for his transgressions before facing death. In a sincere, heartfelt voice, he prayed, "O Lord, by Your grace, we have discovered this treasure, untouched by others. This is a significant accomplishment in our lives, and we are deeply grateful for it. Thank you. Thank you. Thank you."

The moment he uttered "Thank you" for the third time, a miracle happened—the cave door creaked open! His companions stared in astonished disbelief. They soon realized that while the cave's entrance could be accessed from the outside using symbols and clues, the way out was entirely different. It required a password: "Thank you."

The Miracle of Gratitude

This story imparts a profound lesson. When we confront an adverse event and feel sad and hopeless, we find ourselves trapped in the dark cave of negativity. In such moments, we should express gratitude for the event, no matter how challenging it may seem. The door to the treasure trove of joy will surely open. Gratitude aligns us with Nature, transforms our feelings, and elevates our consciousness.

Adding prayer to negative events

When confronted with adverse circumstances, enhance your gratitude through prayer. For instance, if someone deceives you, rather than fixating on the deceit, express gratitude by saying, "One day they will speak the truth, and the truth shall prevail. Thank you for that."

Whenever a negative emotion arises in response to an event, the first step is to greet it with sincere gratitude. For instance, if fear of the future takes hold and fills your mind with thoughts like, "What will happen to my children if I am not around?" start by thanking the fear itself. Then, align yourself with Nature through a constructive prayer: "My future is secure and brimming with the abundance of Nature's blessings." By thanking the negativity that arises from undesirable events, you strengthen your prayer. You must also be grateful for negative feelings because although they are unpleasant, they serve as a mirror, revealing hidden flaws within you and prompting you to seek divine guidance through prayer.

When facing challenges, remind yourself that God has already graced you with countless blessings—opportunities to learn, grow, and evolve. Express heartfelt gratitude for these blessings. Often, when one door closes, countless others open. God constantly guides us with new lessons, steering us toward progress and helping us realize our true essence. No matter how difficult a situation may seem, we cannot comprehend the precious lesson for growth it offers, nor can we perceive the seed of transformation hidden within it. So, we cannot appreciate the positive change it can bring within us. Once we understand this, we can thank God for the grace being constantly showered upon us, not by unquestioningly believing in it but by genuinely knowing it with conviction.

Therefore, when things do not go as planned, embrace the moment and pray with acceptance:

"This task remains unfinished—thank you. Flaws have been pointed out in my work—thank you. Moving forward, every task will flow effortlessly, gracefully, and with exceptional quality—thank you."

When things don't go as planned, many react with anger toward God. Some even lose faith when faced with adversity, declaring, "This proves that God does not exist." Others question, "If God is real, why do so many bad things happen to me? How could He allow this suffering?" People often lose their composure over trivial inconveniences. For instance, if they find themselves stuck in traffic, they may lose their temper and begin cursing the system and those around them. But what if we could shift our perspective? Instead of feeling frustrated, we can choose to be grateful. Tell yourself, "Thank you, God, for this traffic jam. Thank you for this temporary pause. It will clear soon, and I will experience relief and joy. This traffic jam has happened to create this moment of joy!"

The circle of acceptance, prayer, and gratitude

"It's good that it ended here; it could have been worse, but we were spared." This simple yet powerful statement can serve as a life mantra. We all encounter unexpected challenges—accidents, serious illnesses, and other unforeseen events. In such moments, resistance and emotional turmoil often overwhelm us, making it difficult to feel and express gratitude. When faced with such a situation, silently repeat this mantra to yourself. Calm your mind, then surrender the outcome to God, trusting that help will arrive.

Imagine a car damaged in an accident. Instead of focusing on the loss, cultivate gratitude by thinking, "It could have been much worse; only the car was damaged, and we are safe." This shift in perspective empowers us to accept the situation with grace. Acceptance is the first step, and from it, gratitude naturally flows, filling our minds with peace and resilience.

Relationships are among the most precious aspects of our lives, yet circumstances or our state of mind can sometimes strain these vital connections, leading to misunderstandings and painful discord. When relationships falter, we often feel the sting of deep disappointment and question whether they can ever be mended. Negative thoughts and emotions toward the other person may surface, making gratitude seem nearly impossible.

In moments like these, the first step to reclaiming balance is to ground yourself in the present. Pause the spiral of negative thinking—the "what ifs," "how coulds," and "whys." Instead, embrace the situation by thinking, "Thankfully, it stopped here; it could have been much worse, but we were protected."

From this place of acceptance, gratitude begins to flow, empowering you to navigate the aftermath of any loss. A peaceful mind enables you to handle the situation constructively and pray, "May God guide us and help us overcome this setback." As help begins to materialize, your heart will naturally overflow with thankfulness, creating a transformative cycle of acceptance, prayer, and gratitude. This powerful cycle can release you from the suffocating grip of negativity. Let us explore this further with an example.

> Once, two brothers quarreled over the division of their inherited farmland. Though they shared a deep bond, both felt dissatisfied with the division. The younger brother thought, "My elder brother is taking advantage of his age to claim the better land." The elder brother, deeply hurt, resented, "After all the years I've managed this land, he dares to challenge my decisions and disrespect me."

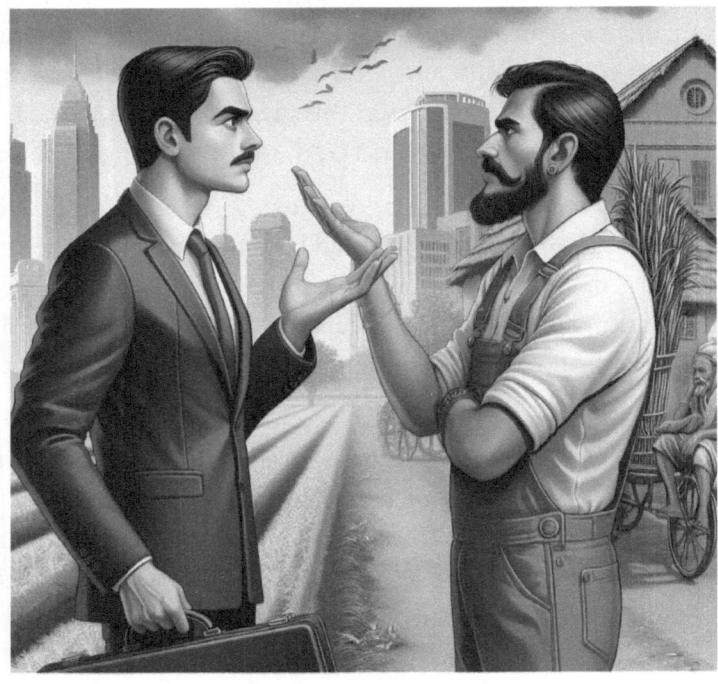

Their conflict escalated to the point where they stopped speaking to each other, weighed down by hurt and anger. Despite their bond, they were engulfed by these negative feelings. Over time, both began to feel uneasy, sensing that something was amiss. Gradually, clarity emerged as each brother reflected on their bond, recalling the love and harmony they had once shared.

The younger brother, living in the city, regularly called to check on his family in the village. The elder brother ensured his younger sibling received fresh produce from the farm and the younger brother always assisted whenever he could. Whenever they met, they enjoyed meals together and cherished each other's company. These memories rekindled the warmth of their connection, revealing the true strength of their bond. What once felt like an insurmountable conflict now seemed like a minor misunderstanding that could be easily resolved through love and open communication.

Once acceptance took root in their hearts, the brothers began recognizing each other's positive qualities. They thought, "In this world, many siblings end up in court over land disputes, yet my brother would never act that way." Both were filled with gratitude.

The younger brother reflected, "Why shouldn't I agree with my elder brother's suggestion? He understands the land much better than I do and would never intentionally give me a bad plot. Even if my share seems smaller, does it really matter? He has managed everything for years, allowing me to enjoy a peaceful life in the city. I should apologize for this misunderstanding and thank him for all he has done."

Meanwhile, the elder brother considered, "I will explain the pros and cons of both fields and let him make the choice. After all, I'll still manage the land; he's not taking it away from me."

In no time, the dark clouds of misunderstanding dissipated, and they forgot that the conflict had ever existed. The issue resolved itself naturally and harmoniously without needing much discussion.

This powerfully illustrates the transformative power of the cycle of acceptance, prayer, and gratitude. When gratitude takes the place of complaints, even the deepest discord can dissolve. In the most challenging situations, a positive and harmonious outcome can emerge.

Points for Contemplation:

- Practice performing prayer when faced with a negative event.
- Write down your understanding of the circle of acceptance, prayer, and gratitude and how you will apply it in any adverse event.

22

Gratitude for Prosperity

"I am grateful for all of my problems. After each one was overcome, I became stronger and more able to meet those that were still to come. I grew in all my difficulties."
- J.C. Penney

Financial difficulties can create a constant sense of scarcity, preoccupying one's thoughts and overshadowing everything else. This mindset of lack often blinds people to the blessings they already have, causing them to erroneously think, "What do I have to be grateful for? I have nothing!"

Gratitude is a transformative force that can shift the experience of scarcity into one of abundance. If you find it challenging to feel grateful, you need to invite gratitude into your life intentionally. Let us explore how to do this.

Find a quiet space where you can sit calmly and reflect on the invaluable blessings that have been bestowed upon you. Then, write them down in a journal or diary.

For instance, if you earn money through a job or business, it does not matter whether the amount is small or large; focus on the fact that your efforts are being rewarded. Start by expressing gratitude in writing: "O God, you have blessed me with wages, rewarding me for my hard work, and for that, I am deeply grateful. Thank you!"

Every day, you share meals with your family. When guests visit, you welcome them warmly and lovingly serve them food. Dining together as a family is one of life's greatest blessings. Remember, countless people around the world have no family and struggle to find even two meals daily.

The next time a plate of food is placed before you, pause and feel grateful for it. Reflect on this blessing and say, "O God, thank you so much for granting me the ability to earn this pure and nourishing food for my family and me. You have blessed me with the capacity to savor this meal. Thank you, thank you, thank you."

We all wear clothes suited to the seasons, such as light cotton in the summer, cozy woolen garments in the winter, and protective raincoats during the monsoons. However, many people lack the luxury of enough clothing to adapt to the changing weather. If you have this privilege, express your heartfelt gratitude: "O God, you fulfill all my clothing needs, protecting me through every season. I am deeply grateful for this gift. Thank you, thank you, thank you."

If your children attend school or college, and you have the means to pay their fees, provide them with books and support their education, ask yourself, "Aren't these signs of prosperity?" and offer your gratitude.

When you go out with your family for a meal, a movie, or a simple outing, remember to thank God. Recognize that you are not only meeting life's needs but are also able to indulge in its joys and pleasures, and for that, always be grateful.

Even in something as routine as transportation—whether you travel by airplane, train, bus, car, scooter, or bicycle—be grateful for the convenience. Say, "O God, thank you for the comfort and ease of travel. I am grateful that I do not have to walk long distances to reach my destination."

In our homes, we all rely on electricity and pay the bill monthly. While this may seem routine, take a moment to express your gratitude: "O God, thank you so much for providing me with the resources to pay my electricity bill on time." Similarly, in our daily lives, we make timely payments for many expenses. Make it a habit to say thank you for each payment you make. Gradually, you will start to feel a sense of abundance, and the flawed notion of wealth your mind may have clung to will begin to dissolve. **True wealth lies in having the means to fulfill your needs without delay—when you need money, it flows to you.**

Reflect on a time when you faced a challenge, perhaps a financial one. Did you seek help from someone, and were they able to support you? Did you feel gratitude? Or perhaps the person you asked declined. Did you feel disappointed or resentful? Then, what if someone else unexpectedly offered the help you needed? Did you express heartfelt thanks, or did you dwell on resentment toward the person who refused earlier?

Recognizing and expressing gratitude for timely help is essential. When you receive assistance, offer your thanks—not only to the individual but also to God, the ultimate orchestrator of grace. Marvel at how Nature often works through unexpected channels to meet your needs. This acknowledgment fills your heart with wonder at the miraculous ways the Universe operates.

You may sometimes worry that your income only covers your expenses, leaving no room for savings, which can make you feel burdened by fears of financial insecurity. However, pause to consider that countless people around the world struggle to meet even their basic daily needs.

Those who embrace gratitude as a way of life often say, "Practice thankfulness," while those consumed by a mindset of scarcity retort, "What is there to be thankful for? I have nothing."

Life sometimes presents situations where one becomes burdened with debt. During such times, one might wonder, "What is there to be thankful for?"

The first step is to **accept** your current reality. **Express gratitude** for the divine will and **pray** with conviction for abundance: "My future will be filled with prosperity." Next, feel grateful to the person or institution that helped you with money or a loan. Resolve and affirm, "I am committed to repaying this debt on time." If repayment is delayed, apologize and reassure the lender that your earnest efforts to repay are ongoing.

Remember, Nature responds to the purity of your intentions and efforts. When your feelings are aligned with pure intentions, your aspirations manifest. However, conflicting emotions, like gladly accepting a loan but resenting the repayment, hinder prosperity. Embrace repayment with gratitude and faith, affirming even before the debt is cleared: "Thank you, God, for allowing me the means to fully repay my debt."

Often, the sense of lack we experience is not rooted in reality but is born out of comparison. Let us understand this with an example.

Shubham was admitted to a prestigious college. His parents paid his tuition, bought him good clothes, and ensured he had everything he needed. He commuted to college on his scooter and was content until he saw a friend arrive in a premium vintage car. Immediately, he felt inadequate, comparing his scooter to the car. This comparison sparked a sense of lack, which only intensified as he continued to compare himself to others.

Next, Shubham noticed a friend with an iPhone and began to imagine how amazing it would be to own one. These comparisons weighed heavily on his mind, and his studies faltered. Resentment crept in and he complained to his parents, feeling like he had nothing and that his life was meaningless.

In this scenario, there is no gratitude, only the turmoil and restlessness born from comparison and pretense. This restlessness is the greatest barrier to prosperity, clouding one's perspective. Obsessed with comparison, one fails to recognize their own abundance, focusing solely on the perceived prosperity of others and yearning to emulate them.

Shifting from comparison to gratitude naturally leads to progress. If Shubham focused on being grateful for attending a reputable college with excellent faculty, placement opportunities, and talented classmates, he would recognize the immense opportunity before him. This gratitude would inspire him to study diligently, achieve his goals, and contribute meaningfully to his family and society. His mind would be at peace, and his perspective would broaden. He might even notice peers commuting by bus or walking, further appreciating his own resources. With this clarity, Shubham could help his friends escape the trap of comparison and pretense, fostering contentment and a sense of purpose.

A Testimonial of Gratitude

After marriage, I moved from a prosperous family to a more modest household. My life changed drastically. While my parents' home had help for all household tasks, I now had to manage everything myself, balancing household duties and expenses. This seemingly simple situation was made special by my response.

Whenever I felt a sense of lack, I expressed gratitude. Having grown up witnessing my family embrace gratitude as a way of life and experience abundance regardless of circumstances, this understanding made it easier for me to express thanks, even in difficult moments.

For instance, instead of lamenting the simplicity of my meals compared to my upbringing, I thanked God for the nourishment. During festivals, I expressed heartfelt gratitude for the chance to wear new clothes, thinking, "I have beautiful clothes to wear to celebrate the occasion."

When enjoying seasonal fruits, I silently thanked Nature, saying, "Thank you for the delicious fruits of this season." Over time, this gratitude transformed not only my mindset but also my circumstances. Today, my life overflows with abundance in every aspect. For this, I am profoundly thankful, knowing that gratitude was the key that unlocked the blessings in my life.

- A seeker of Truth

Certain principles can help transform scarcity into abundance. We must first understand how they work.

It is a universal truth: Where our attention goes, our energy flows. By shifting our focus from "What we don't have" to "What we have," we redirect our energy, transforming it from lack to abundance. Gratitude emerges, and we begin living with a sense of completeness. We welcome prosperity every moment, naturally inviting it into our lives.

Another essential principle for abundance is that **sharing multiplies wealth**. Some think, "How can I share when I barely have enough?" However, everyone has something to give; it is the intention to share that matters.

Begin by cultivating goodwill for the world. Offer a heartfelt prayer for global peace, harmony, and the well-being of all. This act of pure intention becomes a powerful gift of positive energy and serves as a first step in the practice of giving.

When meals are prepared at home, they are rarely made in exact proportions. There is almost always enough food to serve one extra person. If not, make a conscious effort to prepare a little extra. Whenever possible, offer a portion of freshly cooked food to someone in need. Do not let pride or a sense of superiority overshadow your kindness. Let the act of giving be filled with humility and gratitude toward the person who accepts, acknowledging the opportunity they provide you to serve.

Set aside a small amount from your monthly income with the heartfelt intention: "I will use this money for the welfare of others." You can donate it to an organization supporting those in need or directly assist an individual who needs help.

Allocate a small portion of your daily essentials for the betterment of others, and rest assured that you will not incur any loss. On the contrary, the Universe will respond by expanding your capacity to give even more.

This feeling of benevolence enriches the giver, fostering a profound sense of abundance. By integrating the practice of giving a part of your life, you not only enhance your own gratitude but also inspire others to embrace its transformative power. Share your experiences of abundance and gratitude so that others may also invite prosperity into their lives.

Points for Contemplation:

- Do you feel that you have less compared to others? Counter this feeling by expressing gratitude for what you have now.
- Do you realize that true prosperity resides in the mind rather than in the possessions we have? Cultivate gratitude for your wealth and jot it down.
- Do you share with others? What are different ways to share?

23

Attracting Qualities Through Gratitude

"Gratitude makes sweet miracles of small moments."
- Mary Davis

We often judge others based on their outward appearance rather than their character. But consider why figures like Lord Rama, Lord Krishna, Guru Nanak, Jesus, and Prophet Muhammad are revered. Is it for their outward appearances or their exceptional virtues?

Lord Rama is hailed as the epitome of righteousness, Lord Krishna for his divine wisdom, Guru Nanak for his divine utterances, Jesus for his forgiveness, and Prophet Muhammad for his devotion and exemplary conduct.

Ask yourself: What kind of person do you admire? Is it someone dishonest and deceitful, or someone truthful, hardworking, and sincere? The answer is obvious—an honest person. Even a thief seeks a loyal accomplice! So, it is important to cultivate virtues within ourselves. How do we inculcate them, especially if we feel we lack them? Let us explore this through a story:

> Neeraj and Dheeraj worked in the same office. While Dheeraj approached his tasks with joy, enthusiasm, and dedication, Neeraj struggled and felt perpetually stressed. Naturally, Dheeraj's work was consistently praised, which fueled Neeraj's resentment and left him wondering why he couldn't work with the same drive and commitment as Dheeraj.

A similar dynamics played out in a joint family. Geeta, the elder daughter-in-law, was a homemaker, while Sunita, the younger daughter-in-law, worked in an office. Geeta efficiently managed household chores and contributed to the family income through tailoring, while Sunita balanced her career but struggled with domestic responsibilities.

Instead of understanding each other's circumstances, they judged, compared, and blamed each other. Geeta felt Sunita should contribute more at home. At the same time, Sunita thought that since Geeta was at home all day, she should handle the domestic responsibilities, especially given that she returned home exhausted from work. Their comparisons eroded their harmony, causing them to focus only on each other's perceived shortcomings.

Both stories illustrate the negative impact of comparison, resentment, jealousy, and guilt. These emotions lower our consciousness and disconnect us from our true nature. Gratitude, however, reconnects us. We can begin by expressing gratitude for the qualities we wish to cultivate, even before they fully manifest within us.

Neeraj can shift his perspective and appreciate Dheeraj's dedication and strong work ethic by praying, "Thank you, God, for giving me the same wonderful work ethic and enthusiasm that Dheeraj has."

Similarly, Sunita can appreciate Geeta's physical endurance and resilience by saying, "Thank you, God, for giving me the same strength and efficiency that Geeta has." Geeta can appreciate Sunita by saying, "Thank you, God, for giving me opportunities to earn money like Sunita has."

You may wonder how you can be grateful for qualities you don't yet have. Our subconscious mind can't distinguish between what is real and what is imagined. When we express gratitude for something we want, our subconscious accepts it as the truth and starts working to make it happen. Feeling grateful makes us more receptive, helping those things manifest more easily and quickly.

Expressing gratitude before receiving something strengthens our faith, which then acts like a magnet, attracting those very things.

Reflect on your good qualities, list them, and be grateful for each one. This practice strengthens those qualities, naturally reduces negative ones, and helps prevent new negative traits from developing. This practice also makes it easier to notice and appreciate the good in others.

Guru Nanak Dev emphasized the importance of virtues, stating, "Until we have good qualities, we will be swayed by the lure of the illusory world. Developing virtues strengthens our character."

Gautam Maharshi, the renowned Jain saint, praised virtues by stating, "Virtues are incredibly valuable. We receive them through divine grace." Developing virtues is essential. They help us realize our divine nature and bring us happiness, peace, and prosperity. A truly virtuous person seeks virtues not just for worldly success but for true liberation.

In the Bhagavad Gita, Lord Krishna describes the virtues of a devotee in Bhakti Yoga. Embracing these qualities leads to liberation (*Moksha*). We should be grateful for these virtues. Despite being part of the Divine, many of us feel disconnected from these qualities. Gratitude reconnects us to our divine nature, signifying completeness.

From the list of virtues below, choose the qualities you want to develop. Express gratitude for these qualities regularly. This will sow the seeds for these virtues to grow and flourish within you.

Acceptance	Awareness of awareness	Bliss
Commitment	Communication skills	Compassion
Consistency	Contentment	Courage
Creativity	Decision-making	Detachment
Devotion	Empathy	Flexible intellect
Focus	Forgiveness	Friendliness
Gratitude	Honesty	Impersonal living
Infallible faith	Integrity	Mindfulness
Patience	Piousness	Proficiency
Purity of mind	Receptivity	Resilience
Self-discipline	Self-reliance	Selflessness
Simplicity	Skillfulness	Surrender to the Divine
Unconditional love	Virtuous association	Willpower

Points for Contemplation:

- Express gratitude daily for the virtues you observe in your family members.
- At work, recognize and appreciate the good qualities of everyone – colleagues, supervisors, staff, and even the cleaning crew – and thank them.
- When you meet someone new, notice and appreciate one of their good qualities and express gratitude for it.

PART 4

From Gratitude Toward Supreme Gratitude

24

Let Gratitude Become a Way of Life

"Share what you have with others. By consistently giving and being in the feeling of gratitude, you become a powerful channel for abundance."
- Sirshree

One early morning, Grandpa and his young grandson strolled through the park. Admiring the vibrant flowers and lush greenery, Grandpa exclaimed, "Wow! How wonderful!" expressing his gratitude to Nature.

They saw a gardener diligently tending to the plants a short distance away. Grandpa inquired about his well-being, praised his hard work, and thanked him. Nearby, a group of people were practicing yoga. Grandpa paused, watched them intently, and thanked them.

Some children were playing on the other side of the garden, their laughter filling the air. As Grandpa watched them, he thanked them, "Thank you for bringing such happiness and liveliness to the garden." He then gave some money to a destitute woman sitting by the path and thanked her.

Intrigued, the grandson finally couldn't hold himself back. "Grandpa," he asked, "why do you always thank everyone? You thanked the gardener even though he never helped you. You also thanked the flowers and plants for no reason. And what about that yoga group? What have they done for you? You even thanked that poor woman!"

Grandpa chuckled warmly and replied, "I thanked them because they touched my heart. I thanked the flowers and plants as their beauty uplifts our spirits; their fragrance refreshes us and brings us joy. As for the gardener, he nurtures this beauty. His efforts allow the flowers to bloom and the plants to thrive. The people practicing yoga inspire me to take care of my health. The hardship of the destitute woman reminded me of how blessed we are and stirred kindness and compassion within me. This is why I thanked her as well."

The grandson's eyes lit up. "I used to believe that we should only thank those who help us or give us gifts," he said, "but you've opened my eyes to a whole new dimension of gratitude."

Grandpa nodded. "Yes, son, the scope of gratitude is grander than you think. But for today, understand that if someone listens to your woes and pains, you should thank them as they help you unburden your heart. If someone compliments you, thank them as they help you realize that you are a part of this beautiful cosmic creation. You can be thankful for so many things as long as you feel them from the bottom of your heart. For this, you should always remain in a state of love and gratitude. Practice gratitude to such an extent that it becomes an integral part of you. Always be grateful, especially during challenging situations."

The grandson thanked his grandpa for sharing such profound knowledge.

The importance of practicing gratitude has been emphasized and honored in religious and spiritual traditions across various cultures. Many scriptures remind us of the significance of thanking the Divine throughout our daily lives. For instance, thank God upon waking for granting the gift of a new day; gently touch the ground with reverence and thank it before placing your feet on it; offer salutations to water before bathing followed by offering salutations and water to the Sun; express gratitude to God before eating food. These practices reflect our gratitude toward God.

In addition to this, traditions like bathing in sacred rivers, visiting holy places, fasting, praying, performing rituals, lighting lamps and incense, and making offerings help awaken our devotion and cultivate gratitude toward God.

Gratitude Prayer

Let us now embrace the transformative power of gratitude with this prayer.

- God, I am grateful for all the gifts in my life that bring me joy and peace.
- I thank the divine energy that inspires me to move forward every moment.
- I express my heartfelt gratitude to God for enabling me to accomplish every task. I am forever thankful for the blessings bestowed on me.
- I constantly remind myself to be thankful and express gratitude for everything that comes my way. With every breath, I feel more grateful in life.
- Today, I take another step forward in my journey, even if it's a small one. For this little progress, too, I thank God.
- My life is meaningful. I am healthy and happy, and I express my profound gratitude for all these blessings.
- God, I know You are always listening to me, and for this, I am deeply grateful. I thank You for forgiving the mistakes I commit in ignorance and Your guidance that leads me toward a brighter path. I thank You for Your boundless compassion.

- I forgive all those who have wronged or deceived me. I choose positivity, and as I keep my thoughts pure, goodness flows effortlessly into my life.
- The gratitude I express and the sincere words I use to thank others manifest as beautiful truths in my life.
- I dedicate myself to selfless service, helping others with an open heart.
- I believe in the power of giving and hope that, like the saints and sages before us, all people will find joy in serving those in need without expecting anything in return. Truly, there is no greater vision of humanity than this.
- God, thank You for awakening this spirit of selflessness and humanity within us all.
- I am grateful for this Earth, the vast sky, the Universe, and all living beings.
- I cherish the beauty that surrounds me and the experiences that help me evolve into a better version of myself every day.
- Day by day, I make thoughtful decisions to create the ideal life I desire. I am immensely grateful for everything I have and everything I am becoming. I am adorning my life with hope, gratitude, and healing energy.
- With love and acceptance, I embrace good habits that nurture my body, mind, and spirit.
- God, I am ready to embrace my life with an open heart and love, as I know You love me unconditionally. I am immensely grateful for Your eternal love.
- I fully trust that whatever I truly need is already present in my life.
- I thank Your divine force within and around me, inspiring me every moment to move forward, stay strong, and follow the path of truth.

Express your gratitude daily, either verbally or in writing. Writing aligns your thoughts and emotions, deepening their impact. This mindful practice of gratitude opens you to divine blessings and transforms your life.

You can customize this prayer in your own words, adding to it as necessary. Speak or write your personal gratitude prayer daily, making it a way of life.

Points for Contemplation:

- Express gratitude for all the small things from morning till night.
- Appreciate the good habits and qualities in those around you, including your family, friends, neighbors, and colleagues.
- Write the gratitude prayer for yourself.

25

Celebrate Thanksgiving Every Day

"Focus on the goodness you have, for whatever you focus on boosts the power of gratitude. This is how happiness blossoms."
- **Anonymous**

A saint, serenely seated in his room, was discussing something with a group of people when a young man abruptly barged in, kicking the door open. Unperturbed, the saint calmly said to him, "Please step outside and come in again."

The young man was puzzled but thought there must be a reason for the saint's strange request. He complied by stepping out of the room and re-entering in the same manner, pushing the door open with his foot.

The saint, still composed, reiterated his request, "Please step outside and come in again."

This time, the young man hesitated, wondering, "Why is the saint insisting on this?" In that moment of contemplation, he realized his mistake. He gently opened the door with his hand and entered the room politely. The saint smiled and invited him to sit.

In this seemingly minor incident, the saint's mindful behavior conveys a subtle message. The all-pervading consciousness permeates everything in the universe—both living and non-living, still and moving. There is no place devoid of consciousness. Recognizing this truth, we should be grateful for everything. When we express respect and appreciation, we honor the divine all-pervading consciousness.

If your level of awareness is low, you might express gratitude only on festive occasions like Dussehra, Diwali, Christmas, Eid, or other special days. Even then, it may not emerge from the heart but remain a mere ritual.

On the contrary, if you start living in a spirit of gratitude every day, being thankful for every breath, every relationship, comfort, and possession, you will attain the highest state of consciousness. This shift transforms ordinary thankfulness into a profound state of supreme gratitude. In this heightened state, your life becomes a celebration of gratitude, where every moment feels like a sacred thanksgiving.

Points for Contemplation:

- List all your possessions and relationships, acknowledge consciousness within them, and accept them with heartfelt gratitude.
- Pay close attention to the utility and care of inanimate objects, treating them with respect and gratitude, and honoring their contribution to your life.
- Approach your daily chores with thankfulness, making every day a celebration of life.

26

Moving toward Supreme Gratitude

*"Develop an attitude of gratitude.
Say thank you to everyone you meet for everything they do for you."*
- Brian Tracy

Throughout history, great souls have graced the Earth, significantly contributing to the advancement of humanity. Remarkable luminaries like Sage Charaka, the pioneer of Ayurveda, Dr. Samuel Hahnemann, the founder of Homeopathy, and Sage Patanjali, the father of Yoga, made discoveries that continue to benefit humanity even today.

The inventions of numerous scientists have made human life more convenient. Thomas Edison's electric bulb, the Wright brothers' airplane, and Alexander Graham Bell's telephone revolutionized how we live, travel, and communicate.

Great thinkers like Rabindranath Tagore, Aurobindo Ghosh, and Swami Vivekananda served humanity selflessly. Their teachings and exemplary actions continue to inspire and guide us.

The lives of these luminaries are an expression of supreme gratitude because of their extraordinary deeds. Every time we use electricity, technology, or communicate using today's gadgets, we owe them a debt of gratitude.

Delving into the biographies of these extraordinary personalities can inspire us to continually pursue knowledge, explore, and fully unleash our potential to transform our lives into an expression of supreme gratitude.

Humanity has been blessed with the presence of many great saints like Guru Nanak, Buddha, Jesus, Saint Kabir, Saint Meera, Rahim, Ramana Maharshi, and many more. These enlightened beings revealed the profound mysteries of the inner world, guiding people toward liberation from suffering. Their teachings propagated the practices of meditation, devotion, unconditional love, wisdom, renunciation, forgiveness, and surrender, guiding people toward self-realization. These revered saints bestowed upon us sacred scriptures like the Vedas, Quran, Bible, Bhagavad Gita, and Guru Granth Sahib. These timeless texts help people find meaning and purpose in life.

If you are treading the path of truth shown by these enlightened beings with awareness, practicing meditation and devotion, your life can certainly become a divine symphony, much like the music played through a hollow flute, uplifting others.

When life transcends personal desires, when we find joy in the happiness of others, and when our aspirations become selfless, a profound transformation takes root within us. Our thoughts expand beyond the narrow confines of individual concerns, and this power of selfless intentions begins to take the form of a miracle. Over time, our thoughts, feelings, speech, and actions get infused with the sacred feeling of welfare for all beings. Expressions of heartfelt gratitude to God blossom in the core of our being, radiating auspicious vibrations of supreme gratitude.

When divine virtues like compassion, kindness, unconditional love, unwavering faith, joy, wonder, veneration, and inner silence begin to bloom within us, the mind becomes loving, pure, and resolute. This leads to a divinely blessed life that seamlessly progresses toward the state of supreme gratitude.

If we aspire to elevate gratitude to its supreme form, we must understand the truth of life and embrace each moment with faith and surrender, allowing this transformation to reach the depths of our subconscious mind. Such a transformed life is indeed a life of supreme gratitude.

Let us take a moment to reflect on the following questions:

- Do I want to continue living the way I have until today, or should I strive to awaken and transform my life both inwardly and outwardly?

- Many saints, philosophers, and scientists have lived extraordinary lives of supreme gratitude. The same opportunity is presented to me now. Do I wish to seize it and transform my life into one of supreme gratitude?

If, after honest contemplation, your answer is a heartfelt "Yes," then this is the moment to make a firm resolution and chart a plan to transform this vision into reality.

As life progresses from mere gratitude to supreme gratitude, its significance, value, and sense of fulfillment expand greatly. What wisdom can guide us toward such profound transformation, both inwardly and outwardly?

Wisdom of the true purpose of human life

It is said that one attains a human birth only after evolving through 8.4 million life forms. What a rare and extraordinary gift this human life is! Let us first offer our deepest gratitude to God for blessing us with this unparalleled opportunity.

In this world, it is necessary to earn a livelihood for a comfortable and secure life. Many aim to become doctors, engineers, teachers, lawyers, and so on, dedicating themselves to these pursuits with unwavering determination. Their hard work often bears fruit, and they achieve their aspirations. However, amidst this worldly success, one must pause and ask: Is livelihood alone the ultimate purpose of life?

When the pursuit of a livelihood aligns with the real purpose of life on Earth*, it transcends mere existence and becomes the Complete Goal. Our real purpose on Earth is to train the mind to develop the qualities of steadfastness, integrity, purity, and love. By embracing this inner transformation, our life becomes effortless, simple, profoundly meaningful, and powerful. This is the path that leads us from gratitude to supreme gratitude.

Points for Contemplation:

- According to you, what is the real purpose of this birth on Earth?
- What different qualities of mind do you possess? Which one needs to be instilled? How will you develop new qualities?

---

*To delve deeper into the real purpose of life on Earth, read the book "The Soul Purpose" by Sirshree.

27

Surrender, Fulfillment, and Gratitude

"There is a calmness to a life lived in gratitude, a quiet joy."
- Ralph H. Blum

A king once invited a mystic to dine at his palace. On the appointed day, the mystic arrived, dressed in his usual simple attire. However, the palace guards, judging him by his humble clothing, refused to believe that the king had invited him and denied him entry into the palace. Without protest, the mystic quietly returned home.

The following day, the king sent another invitation, urging the mystic to join him for a meal. This time, the mystic borrowed an elegant suit and wore it to the palace. Upon his arrival, the guards greeted him with respect, promptly informed the king of his arrival, and escorted him to the royal dining hall with great honor.

When the meal was served, the mystic did something unexpected—he began smearing the food on his fine suit. Perplexed, the king inquired, "Why are you staining your suit with food?" With serene composure, the mystic replied, "I am feeding this suit, for it was the suit, not me, that was granted entry into your palace. I had come yesterday, too, but due to my simple attire, I was turned away."

This story speaks profoundly about the human condition. Just as the mystic's attire was valued more than him, humans too often give undue importance to their physical form due to their ignorant belief of "I am this body." While maintaining the body is essential, most people indiscriminately indulge in sense gratification, vainly pursuing the fleeting pleasures of the mind and senses like chasing after a mirage. In this pursuit, they serve only their ego, the notional individual "I" that arises due to identification with the body.

The individualistic ego walks through life with a mental shopping list, constantly seeking what it believes it needs: "I want love, respect, wealth, status, and recognition." It seeks these in its relationships, friendships, and acquaintances, but it fails to grasp the true essence of love and respect.

The turning point comes with a deep thirst to know oneself, a yearning to understand "Who am I?" Then, one embarks on a quest for the truth. When one receives the wisdom of the ultimate truth, one's understanding deepens. Then, one realizes that the body is not who one truly is; it is just a medium to experience the divine consciousness (Self, God, Ishwar, Allah) within. In this realization, life finds true fulfillment and becomes truly successful.

In this journey of life, if the human body is considered like a car or a scooter, what kind of fuel should we fill it with? It must be fueled with truth: listening to the truth, reading about the truth, contemplating it, meditating on it, and cultivating devotion. Conversely, if the human vehicle is fueled by the ego, the constant chatter of "I, me, mine," it will sputter and emit the smoke of discord, the stench of arrogance, and the noise of struggle.

While there is growing concern worldwide about environmental pollution caused by carbon-emitting vehicles, the far more poisonous smoke spewed by the human ego is often overlooked. This invisible smoke, laden with hatred, envy, arrogance, and the constant need to be "right," chokes the collective mental atmosphere. When this pollution dissipates, when ignorance gives way to awareness, unconditional love blossoms and true gratitude emerges. The human form then serves as a mirror to reflect the divine nature of the true Self, and life evolves into a radiant state of supreme gratitude.

The day one truly understands their purpose on Earth, recognizes the intricate arrangements beautifully designed to support them, and perceives every incident as an opportunity for growth, life transforms into a state of supreme gratitude.

When the mind becomes pure, loving, obedient, and steadfast, the body serves as a mirror for the Self to know itself. When the ego surrenders to the divine will, the underlying oneness of all creation becomes evident, giving a profound sense of completeness. In this sublime state, the body is used as a medium to understand and venerate the mysteries of the formless and the embodiment. The depth and significance of grace are fully understood. Only gratitude remains, and a life lived in such a state is an expression of supreme gratitude.

Gratitude – the gateway to fulfillment

When completion is attained with something, some express their gratitude through prayer, while others perceive gratitude itself as prayer. Yet, there is a profound distinction between these approaches. When you express gratitude not after a desire is fulfilled but beforehand, it demonstrates unwavering faith. When such faith nurtures a feeling of completeness within, the very thing you have been thankful for naturally manifests in your life.

For instance, if you aspire to develop the quality of consistency, you can express gratitude in advance, saying, "O God, I am deeply thankful to you for instilling the qualities of consistency and persistence within me."

Similarly, if a prayer arises within you, "May my mind be cleansed of all impurities," affirm your faith with gratitude: "My prayer is already fulfilled; my mind is pure and sanctified. For this, I am profoundly grateful." This gratitude stems from a sense of completeness. However, when gratitude is offered with doubt or a sense of lack, you lack the required strength.

Your body serves as both a transmitter and a receiver. The quality of transmission and reception depends entirely on its inner state. When gratitude flows from a deep sense of completeness, it attracts completeness into every facet of your life. As this understanding takes root, gratitude arises naturally from the wellspring of completeness within you. Life transforms into an endless celebration of supreme gratitude.

Points for Contemplation:

- Please observe your mind. Is it pure, loving, obedient, and steadfast in every incident? If not, what understanding does it need to receive?
- Contemplate "Am I this body?" If not, who am I?
- Express gratitude beforehand for the qualities you want in life.

28

Meditation on Reasons for Gratitude

"Let us rise and be grateful, for if we did not learn a lot today, at least we learned a little. And if we did not learn even a little, at least we did not fall ill. And if we did fall ill, at least we did not die. So, let us all be grateful"
- **Buddha**

We have delved deeply into the essence of gratitude, yet some questions might still linger in the mind. This is natural, as doubts often persist until it is clearly realized at the level of experience. Until we experience it directly, it can be difficult to believe.

Now, let us continue this miraculous journey by practicing meditation on the reasons for gratitude.

Meditation on the reasons for gratitude

Before you begin, read the following steps thoroughly. You can even record them in your own voice for guided practice. When you are ready, proceed with the meditation.

- Select a tranquil, undisturbed spot where you can meditate peacefully. Sit comfortably in a relaxed posture and close your eyes.

- Begin by observing the present state of your body. Notice any tension, heaviness, or discomfort you may be experiencing physically. Then, turn your attention to your mental state, observing any confusion, fear, or doubt. Finally, assess your overall state on a scale of one to ten, where one represents the lowest point, and ten signifies a state of deep relaxation and peace.

- Now, consider your emotional openness. If you feel entirely closed off, rate yourself 1 or 2. If you are open and receptive, assign yourself 8 to 10. A neutral stance, neither open nor closed, would be around 5. A slight openness warrants 6 or 7, while a state of mechanical existence or a lack of awareness would suggest 3 or 4. In this way, examine your internal state minutely.

- Observe how your emotions impact your physical state. For example, when you say, "I am sad," notice how your body tends to constrict. Conversely, when you think, "I am happy," you often feel a sense of expansion and openness. Keeping this in mind, first, assess your current emotional state with the goal of moving beyond your present rating.

- Now, observe how your environment is affecting your body. Do you feel lightness or heaviness in the atmosphere? Are you experiencing a sense of openness or constriction in response? Avoid labelling these sensations as right or wrong; simply observe their effect on you.

- Turn your attention to the rhythm of your breath. Is it slow or rapid, steady or uneven, shallow or deep?

- Raise both hands high, inhale deeply, and exhale slowly. Repeat it two or three times. As you lower your hands, notice the impact this exercise has on your breathing. Did your breath flow freely? Regardless of the outcome, express gratitude for the breath itself. It is the life force, energizing every cell and organ. Offer your gratitude to Nature, to the Divine that sustains you constantly. Also, acknowledge and thank all forms of support in your life, both visible and invisible.

- Shift your focus to any complaints that may be arising within you. Are there complaints about the environment? Perhaps it is too hot, too cold, or simply uncomfortable? Are you experiencing discomfort with your seat, finding it too soft or too hard? Is there any physical pain causing uneasiness? Express gratitude for all these complaints as well.

- Notice how well your body supports you during meditation. Your hands, feet, eyes, ears, nose, tongue, heart, brain, and all other organs are functioning in harmony. Any pain or discomfort serves as feedback from these organs. You are receiving feedback, which signifies that your body is functioning effectively. The intensity of this feedback varies among individuals; it may be subtle or pronounced, minimal or substantial. Regardless of the feedback you receive, express gratitude for it.

- Touch each part of your body with loving kindness, offering sincere thanks. Gratitude possesses the power to open those areas within you that feel constricted.

- Express gratitude for both your successes and failures in life. It is essential to thank your failures as well, for they have provided invaluable lessons that have guided you on your journey.

- Now, reflect on these questions: "What lessons am I learning from my failures? Who am I? What qualities are being expressed through me? At this moment, the quality of gratitude is being expressed. I am grateful for being able to express gratitude."

- Observe which thoughts create a sense of openness and which ones cause you to withdraw. What aspects of the world trigger a constricted feeling? Ask yourself, "Am I open or closed right now? What can I do to open up?" Then, by cultivating a feeling of gratitude, become thankful and allow yourself to open.

- Raise your hands and bring the feeling of "letting go" into your awareness. Release every complaint held within. There is no need to confine the "birds" of complaints within the "cage" of your body. Visualize them flying away freely, expressing gratitude. You, too, thank them for awakening you. Having received your lessons, express gratitude for your complaints, saying, "You are free, and so am I. Thank you for awakening me!"

- Even if you feel resistance in expressing gratitude, consciously practice it. Allow the best things intended for you to easily flow into your life, according to the divine plan. Let the constricted mind, which resists gratitude for any reason, open up to this fundamental truth: What you give returns, multiplied. Continue to open yourself to the feeling of gratitude. What you have not yet received is also playing a role, clearing unnecessary obstacles and awakening you to new insights.

- Often, we are unaware of what in our lives diverts us from our ultimate earthly purpose. For some, wealth becomes a distraction from truth, while for others, it serves as a guide toward it. Everything happening in your life is ultimately leading you toward truth; express gratitude for it. There is hidden grace in what you have not received. Give yourself a moment to reflect, asking, "How have I benefited from not receiving this?" or "Due to this sorrowful incident, what qualities have emerged within me? Can I be thankful for this?"

- If you have experienced a lack of love in your life, what might be the underlying reason? By not receiving love, you are being guided to become a source of love. Nature is working to bestow this grace upon you; imagine the depth of gratitude you owe for this profound lesson!

- If your health is less than ideal, find a reason for gratitude. Your body is your friend, and its illness offers an opportunity to realize that you are not solely defined by it. You can express your true self even within the body's limitations. You are being given an opportunity to raise the consciousness of others through your example. Beyond these, identify other reasons for expressing gratitude, consciously acknowledge them, and offer thanks.

- Discover your flaws and their causes so that daily complaints can be transformed into genuine gratitude. Release all complaints, embracing a life free from them. When you are grateful, even your perceived lacks in life become powerful sources of insight.

- If you find yourself complaining about your children, reflect on why these souls were entrusted to you. Each one has their own journey, and their presence will awaken and help you grow. Their existence opens you to the experience of unconditional love. So, will you dwell on complaints or choose to express gratitude? Tell yourself, "I am open to change. Even if I am resistant now, I can choose to open up. I can recall and be grateful for all that I already have."

- Take a moment to appreciate what you hold: Eyes that witness the divine beauty of the world, ears that capture its harmonious sounds. A nose that breathes life-giving air and savors countless scents, and a tongue that tastes diverse flavors, nurturing your well-being.

- Your face reflects the divine countenance; your hands enable you to work; your legs allow you to move; your body serves as a medium for your unique expression. You have a home to shelter you, relationships that enrich you, a loving and supportive family, friends to uplift your spirit, art to inspire you, and endless avenues for joy and fulfillment.

- What has been withheld from you? The Earth beneath upholds you. The sky above offers its ever-changing beauty across seasons. Nature's benevolence gifts you with the air you breathe, the water that's vital for your survival, and food that nourishes you. The marvel of modern gadgets—tools that enable you to learn, write, create, and connect; machines that simplify your labor; and vehicles that transport you with ease. All of this exists for you. Consider how blessed life is.

- Feel the warmth of your family, their joy lighting up your life. Picture the smiles of loved ones and the playful laughter of children, the affection of pets, and relatives who stand by you through both joy and sorrow. All these are blessings to be thankful for.

- You are graced with wisdom, devotion, and the gift of selfless service, finding joy in giving. Your prayers are nearing their answers, with many more blessings yet to unfold. Express gratitude for the pure and higher aspirations of growth and awakening, for without them, you would have lived a life of complaints in the illusion of Maya, leaving this world without awakening to the truth. Let gratitude saturate your being.

- You have been given tears of devotion, love for truth, hope for freedom, the ability to listen to wisdom, the habit of contemplation, and the yearning for the ultimate liberation. Offer thanks for all you have received and even for what has not been received. Let every cell resonate with gratitude, sending out ripples of thankfulness until the very air vibrates with gratitude: Thank you… Thank you… Thank you…

- With a sense of deep gratitude, gently lift your hands. Inhale deeply, then exhale slowly. Open your arms wide, extending that feeling of thankfulness into the space around you. After a while, slowly lower your hands.

- Now, on a scale of one to ten, assess the feeling of openness within your body and mind. Reflect on your current state.

- Maintain this feeling of gratitude as you gently open your eyes without rubbing or cupping them. With open eyes, inhale deeply, exhale slowly, and feel the liberation as you express gratitude.

Gratitude! Gratitude!! Gratitude!!!

29

The Gratitude Mantra, Bank, and Journal

"When we express gratitude for even the most trivial events in life, we indeed experience profound joy, no matter how ordinary it may seem."

- Sirshree

Having understood the deep meaning of gratitude, let us now explore why and how to keep a gratitude journal.

By consistently writing down the things we are grateful for in a daily gratitude journal, we gradually cultivate a positive and creative mindset.

The Gratitude Mantra

"O God, fill me not with pride but with overflowing indebtedness. Make my life not heavy with burden, but light with gratitude."

The Gratitude Bank

A piggy bank

An empty jar

A small box

Steps to cultivate the gratitude bank:

1. Pick one of the items shown above and label it as "Gratitude Bank."
2. Write a note that says, "My Gratitude bank account is now open.

Thank you, Thank you, Thank you!" Fold it up and deposit it in your Gratitude bank.

3. Each time you feel grateful, jot it down and put the note in your Gratitude bank.

4. When you are sad or stressed, open your Gratitude bank and read these gratitude notes. They will remind you of all the blessings in your life.

Let us explore how to express gratitude for various aspects of life in the Gratitude journal.

Writing gratitude for everything in life

We are blessed with five sensory organs—nose to smell, ears to hear, eyes to see, tongue for taste, and skin for touch—and five organs of action—mouth to speak, arms to grasp, legs to move, excretory organs for elimination, and reproductive organs for procreation. These faculties enable us to truly experience life in its entirety. So, express gratitude for each, with specific reasons, like this:

"I am grateful for my nose, which enables me to breathe and differentiate between fragrances and foul odors."

....
....
....
....

Only Gratitude!

Point for Contemplation:

- Express gratitude for your eyes, ears, tongue, skin, hands, feet, family, virtues, and ultimately the gift of life itself. Commit to writing at least one heartfelt line of gratitude in your journal every day, acknowledging these blessings.

30

A Gratitude Letter from the Future You

"To harness the transformative power of gratitude and lead a truly successful life, raise both your hands and proclaim: "I am deeply grateful for everything I've received in life. Thank you, Thank you, Thank you!"
- **Sirshree**

When we reflect on our present moment, two scenarios often emerge:

- First, we see the rewards of past good deeds: exercising, eating well, meditating, reading inspiring content, building strong relationships, and praying. These positive actions are now paying off.

- Second, we see the consequences of past mistakes or broken promises, which we now regret.

While the first situation is satisfying, we naturally want to avoid the second. We all wish to act today in ways that guarantee a joyful tomorrow.

A good way to stay grateful is to envision your most evolved future state, the life you truly want, and then examine your current actions in light of this vision.

Ask yourself: What choices am I making today? How disciplined am I? Closely examine your daily life: What are you eating, and who are you spending time with? What habits and interests are you building? What are you reading, listening to, watching, and learning? Think about your mental state, finances, happiness, peace, and how satisfied you feel. Consider your understanding of life and the strength of your relationships.

Essentially, ask yourself: What will my life look like in ten years? What am I doing today to create the future I want?

To truly reach your highest potential, write a heartfelt letter of gratitude to your current self, as if it is coming from your fully evolved and successful future self. This is how you can let it flow:

"I am so grateful to myself for the unwavering support and commitment I gave myself. Because I focused on self-improvement, my natural strengths blossomed, and I could let go of limiting beliefs and habits. I immersed myself in the truth of life—listening, reading, contemplating, and studying it. I diligently worked on every aspect of my life: body, mind, relationships, finances, and spiritual growth. This wholehearted effort has brought me to a life filled with love, joy, peace, completeness, and contentment."

When we say thank you, it is important to explain why. Many people express gratitude without giving a reason. Similarly, people often apologize with a simple "sorry" without specifying what they are apologizing for. An apology is more effective when it names the specific mistake. The same applies to gratitude. So, when you thank your past self from your future perspective, be clear about the particular choices and efforts that led to your happy and fulfilling life.

Picture yourself in the future, filled with joy. From that place, you will thank your present self, saying, "Because of you, I am experiencing this incredible day where everything is in perfect harmony, a world of pure love and happiness. I am deeply grateful for your discipline, consistency, and determination. Your dedication and unwavering love made all this possible. Just like a mother's tireless devotion to her child, your love and devotion worked miracles in my life."

This practice of future gratitude can truly build a brighter tomorrow. It begins with self-love. When you cultivate self-love, you naturally choose exercise and *Pranayama* (breathing exercises) over entertainment and distractions, a healthy and balanced diet, and mindful fasting over cravings and fleeting indulgences. Your consistent practice improves your skills and refines your character.

Thanking yourself this way directs all your energy toward your goals. That's the power of focused intention.

Picture yourself ten years in the future, experiencing a life full of health, happiness, peace, contentment, prosperity, love, and harmony. Now, reflect on your current choices. Express gratitude for both the positive actions you are taking and the negative ones you are consciously avoiding. Here are some examples:

What Is Happening	What Is Not Happening	Gratitude
Exercise	Addictions	Thank you
Treating food as medicine	Succumbing to cravings	Thank you
Pranayama, Meditation	Laziness, unhealthy tendencies	Thank you
Training the mind	Being stubborn and a slave to the mind	Thank you
Reading and Learning	Intellectual stagnation	Thank you

Working on building the foundation of a strong character	Focusing only on polishing one's external appearances	Thank you
Mindful financial investments	Reckless or impulsive spending	Thank you
Meditating on "Who am I?"	Indulging in sensory pleasures	Thank you
Nurturing a platform for open and loving communication in relationships	Insensitivity and bitterness in relationships	Thank you
Being sensitive and responding to people's idea of love	Operating with a fixed "You become like me" attitude	Thank you
Developing skills	Incompetence and procrastination	Thank you
Nurturing creativity	Slave to conventions and fixated ways	Thank you
Persistent effort	Blaming fate and giving up	Thank you
Cultivating inner strength	Blaming circumstances and others	Thank you
Refining virtues	Focusing on flaws	Thank you
Possibility thinking	Limited and blind thinking	Thank you
Transforming past memories	Dwelling on the past and resenting it	Thank you

From today onward, fill yourself with hope and faith in the bright future you are creating, and stay focused on making it a reality. Remember, nothing unfolds in life by chance. Things happen according to the law of karma, which is why conscious actions are so important. Gratitude and awareness are deeply connected. As your awareness rises, your gratitude grows. Hence, it is said, "Live in gratitude and flow with it."

Letter of Gratitude

Thanks to myself for creating this amazing regal life beyond anything I imagined. I am now able to maintain my life in perpetual happiness. I see everything with love, understanding, and good intentions. My best qualities shine through in everything I do. I see the beauty and grandeur of life every day, everywhere, and it brings me true joy. I am profoundly grateful for this healthy and active body.

I have become skilled in concentration, observation, and decision making. I have learned to see life with endless possibilities. I can handle both joy and sorrow with equanimity. Every action I take feels like a form of worship. By accepting people as they are, I have transformed my life into a continuous expression of supreme gratitude.

I receive everything I need at the perfect time. I have become self-sufficient and can help others in the best way. My relationships are harmonious and filled with love and support.

I manage all my belongings well, whether it is my car, phone, or anything else. Thank you for giving me that confidence. I am respected by everyone, and my inner peace is clearly evident. My mind is always open, courageous, and honest. I am pure and sacred, and so is everyone else. In every circumstance, I am able to appreciate that we all are part of God.

Only those thoughts that lead to liberation arise within me. My spiritual growth and my worldly occupation are in perfect balance and harmony. I am using my body, this precious gift, to its fullest potential. I am developing compassion, empathy, love, and creative thinking, understanding that compassion is love in action and gratitude is its supreme expression. I surrender all my actions to the Divine Source of the universe.

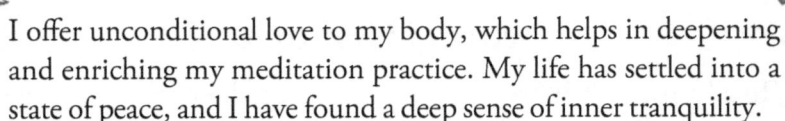

I offer unconditional love to my body, which helps in deepening and enriching my meditation practice. My life has settled into a state of peace, and I have found a deep sense of inner tranquility.

I am diligently working to purify my mind. I am happy and helping others find happiness too. I am able to observe my thoughts with detached awareness. My inner light guides me. On the screen of my mind, the "The Joy of Liberation" movie plays constantly. I enjoy this state of supreme freedom every moment. My devotion has awakened, freeing me from the influence of worldly illusion. I stay balanced through ups and downs. All my delusions have gradually disappeared.

Every day, I see my qualities improving. I can now grasp Nature's signals. My deepening meditation allows me to transcend my fears. I have broken free from limiting thoughts and now live with the feeling, "Everything is possible; everything is abundant and available to everyone." I thank God for making this life a continuous expression of supreme gratitude.

That's all for today. We will meet again, keep meeting and reading these letters from the self to the self.

With boundless gratitude... infinite gratitude... gratitude for supreme gratitude!

Point for Contemplation:

- Write a letter of gratitude to yourself from the future self and read it periodically.

❖ ❖ ❖

You can mail your opinion or feedback on this book to: books.feedback@tejgyan.org

About Sirshree

Sirshree's spiritual quest, which began during his childhood, led him on a journey through various schools of philosophy and meditation practices. He studied a wide range of literature on mind science and spirituality. After a long period of deep contemplation on the truth of life, his quest culminated in attaining the ultimate truth.

Sirshree espouses, "All spiritual paths that lead to the truth begin differently but culminate at the same point – Understanding. This understanding is complete in itself. Listening to this understanding is enough to attain the Truth." Over the last two decades, he has dedicated his life to raise mass consciousness.

Sirshree has delivered more than 4000 discourses that throw light on this understanding. He has designed a system for wisdom, which makes it accessible to all. This system has inspired people from all walks of life to progress on their journey of the Truth. Thousands of seekers join in a virtual prayer for World Peace and Global Healing daily at 9:09 am and 9:09 pm.

About Tej Gyan Foundation

Tej Gyan Foundation is a non-profit organization founded on the teachings of Sirshree. The Foundation disseminates Tejgyan – the wisdom that guides one from self-development to Self-realization, leading towards Self-stabilization.

The Foundation's system for imparting wisdom has been assessed by international quality auditors and accredited with the ISO 9001:2015 certification. This wisdom has been presented in a simple, systematic, and practically applicable form that makes it accessible to people from all walks of life, regardless of religion, caste, social strata, country, or belief system.

The Foundation has centers in more than 400 cities and towns across India and other countries. The mission of Tej Gyan Foundation is to create a highly evolved society by leading seekers from negative thoughts to positive thoughts and further, from positive thoughts to Happy thoughts. A 'Happy thought' is the auspicious thought of being free from all thoughts, leading to the state of supreme bliss beyond thoughts.

If you seek such wisdom that leads you beyond mere knowledge, dissolves all problems, frees you from all limiting beliefs, reveals the true nature of divinity, and establishes you in the ultimate truth, then it is time to discover Tejgyan; it is time to rise above the mundane knowledge of words and experience Tejgyan!

The MahaAasmani Magic of Awakening Retreat

Self-development to Self-realization towards Self-stabilization

Do you wish to experience unconditional happiness that is not dependent on any reason? Happiness that is permanent and only increases with time? Do you wish to experience love, peace, self-belief, harmony in relationships, prosperity, and true contentment? Do you wish to progress in all facets of your life, viz. physical, mental, social, financial, and spiritual?

If you seek answers to these questions and are thirsty for the ultimate truth, then you are welcome to participate in the MahaAasmani Magic of Awakening retreat organized by Tej Gyan Foundation. This is the Foundation's flagship retreat based on the teachings of Sirshree.

The purpose of this retreat

The purpose of this retreat is that every human being should:

- Discover the answer to "Who am I" and "Why am I?" through direct experience and be established in ultimate bliss.

- Learn the art of living in the present, free from the burden of the past and the anxiety of the future.

- Acquire practical tools to help quieten the chattering mind and dissolve problems.

- Discover missing links in the practices of Meditation (*Dhyana*), Action (*Karma*), Wisdom (*Gyana*), and Devotion (*Bhakti*).

About Books by Sirshree

Sirshree's published work includes more than 150 book titles, some of which have been translated into more than 10 languages. His literature provides a profound reading on various topics of practical living and unravels the missing links in karma, wisdom, devotion, meditation, and consciousness.

His books have been published by leading publishing houses like Penguin, Hay House, Bloomsbury, Wisdom Tree, Jaico, etc. "The Source" book series, authored by Sirshree, has sold over 10 million copies. Various luminaries and celebrities like His Holiness the Dalai Lama, publishers Mr. Reid Tracy, Ms. Tami Simon and Yoga Master Dr. B. K. S. Iyengar have released Sirshree's books and lauded his work.

The Source
Attain Both, Inner Peace
and Worldly success

Awaken the Power of Faith
Discover the 7 Principles of the
Highest Power of the Universe

To order books authored by Sirshree, login to:
www.gethappythoughts.org
For further details, call: +91 9011013210

SELECT BOOKS AUTHORED BY SIRSHREE

To order these and other books authored by Sirshree
Visit **www.gethappythoughts.org**

Tej Gyan Foundation – Contact details

Registered Office:
Happy Thoughts Building, Vikrant Complex, Near Tapovan Mandir, Pimpri, Pune 411017, INDIA. Contact: +91 20-27411240, +91 20-27412576

MaNaN Ashram:
Survey No. 43, Sanas Nagar, Nandoshi Gaon, Kirkatwadi Phata, Off Sinhagad Road, Taluka Haveli, Pune district - 411024, INDIA. Contact: +91 992100 8060.

WORLD PEACE PRAYER

Divine Light of Love, Bliss, and Peace is Showering;
The Golden Light of Higher Consciousness is Rising;
All negativity on Earth is Dissolving;
Everyone is in Peace and Blissfully Shining;
O God, Gratitude for Everything!

Members of Tej Gyan Foundation have been offering this impersonal mass prayer for many years. Those who are happy can offer this prayer. Those feeling low or suffering from illness can receive healing with this prayer.

If you are feeling troubled or sick, please sit to receive the healing effect of this prayer. Visualize that the divine white healing light is being showered on earth through the prayers of thousands and is also reaching you, bringing you peace and good health. You can dwell in this feeling for some time and then offer your gratitude to those offering the prayer.

A Humble Appeal

More than a million peace lovers pray for World Peace and Global Healing every morning and evening at 9:09. Also, a prayer (in Hindi) to elevate consciousness is webcast every day on YouTube at 3:30 pm and 9:00 pm IST. Please participate in this noble endeavor.

www.ingramcontent.com/pod-product-compliance
Lightning Source LLC
LaVergne TN
LVHW041840070526
838199LV00045BA/1364